D0733882

UNDERSTANDING
TEENAGE
DEPRESSION

UNDERSTANDING

TEENAGE

DEPRESSION

A GUIDE TO DIAGNOSIS, TREATMENT, AND MANAGEMENT

Maureen Empfield, M.D., and Nicholas Bakalar

An Owl Book
Henry Holt and Company | New York

Henry Holt and Company, LLC
Publishers since 1866
115 West 18th Street
New York, New York 10011

Henry Holt® is a registered trademark of
Henry Holt and Company, LLC.

Library of Congress Cataloging-in-Publication Data
Empfield, Maureen.
 Understanding teenage depression : a guide to diagnosis, treatment,
and management / Maureen Empfield and Nicholas Bakalar.—1st ed.
  p. cm.
 "An Owl book."
 Includes bibliographical references and index.
 ISBN 0-8050-6761-2 (pb)
 1. Depression in adolescence—Popular works. I. Bakalar, Nick. II. Title.
RJ506.D4 E47 2001   2001024104
616.85'27'00835—dc21

Henry Holt books are available for special promotions and
premiums. For details contact: Director, Special Markets.

First Edition 2001

Designed by Betty Lew

Printed in the United States of America

1 3 5 7 9 10 8 6 4 2

To our children

CONTENTS

ACKNOWLEDGMENTS

The idea for this book came from our agent, Richard Balkin, the source of many good ideas and much else of value as well. Isela Puello was tireless and uncomplaining in the face of our ceaseless demands for more research material. Francine Cournos, M.D., our partner in more ways than one, read the entire manuscript with great care, offering invaluable suggestions, corrections, and clarifications. The following people were generous with their knowledge: James Bakalar, J.D., Ewald Horwath, M.D., Marguerite Mayers, M.D., Karen McKinnon, M.A., Howell Schrage, M.D., Peggy Stallman, M.S.W., and Janet Williams, D.S.W. Erin Clermont copyedited the manuscript with conscientious determination and a sharp eye for every detail. We are deeply indebted to our editor, Deborah Brody, for her clear understanding of our goals and her sharp intelligence in helping us achieve them. Perhaps the most important contributors to this effort are the anonymous and semianonymous young men and women whose stories you will read, often in their own words, in this book. To them our heartfelt thanks for their wisdom, and our profound admiration for their courage in the face of terrible pain.

PREFACE

Imagine this: you're 16 years old and you're doing poorly in school because you can't get yourself to concentrate on anything. Your girlfriend dumped you because she could no longer tolerate your bad moods, and the people who used to be your friends are avoiding you, for which you can't really blame them since you're moping all the time. It looks like you'll probably flunk at least two subjects this semester, and you have no idea what you're going to do next. No activity, even those you used to like, seems interesting; everything seems empty, pointless. You can't see any way out, or any possible satisfactory future. In addition to these desperate feelings, you are exhausted all the time and can't sleep properly. You sometimes feel nauseated, and food doesn't taste right. There is a persistent sinking feeling in your stomach, as if something even more terrible is about to happen. You keep getting headaches that won't go away. The slightest noise seems painfully loud. You're squirming when you try to sit still, but at the same time you feel too tired for physical activity. Although you are sure you must once have felt happy, you can no longer remember the feeling, and you are convinced you will never again feel any different from the way you feel right now.

Can you imagine all that? A teenager suffering from major depression can actually feel even worse than what you are now imagining.

Many people still believe that depression, and especially teenage depression, is not really a disease, that a youngster who is persistently and irrationally sad, uncommunicative, deliberately withdrawn and isolated, angry, irritated, or overly sensitive to criticism is just suffering ordinary "growing pains" and should pull herself together, snap out of it, and get on with growing up. "A good kick in the pants," some say, is all a teenager needs to get put back on the right track.

Unfortunately, this is not so. Clinical depression, which entails a number of extremely debilitating physical and psychological symptoms that we discuss at length in this book, is a serious disease that can do terrible and even permanent damage to a teenager's developmental progress. Like other serious diseases, it requires professional attention, with treatments that are both medical and psychological. Failing to treat the illness when it occurs can have dreadful consequences, up to and including death by suicide. Telling a youngster with major depression to "just shape up and get on with it" is about as helpful as giving the same advice to a youngster with a broken leg. It is bad advice, with a high potential for a disastrous outcome.

We all feel sad from time to time, and even perfectly healthy teenagers, faced with the very real problems of finding a place in an adult world that still seems in many ways mysterious, may feel sad more often, or more acutely, than healthy adults. But clinical depression is another matter entirely. It is not just feeling sad or a little blue. It is an overwhelming feeling of hopelessness and despair that can be accompanied by severe physical symptoms including lack of appetite, inability to sleep, physical aches and pains, complete exhaustion, digestive problems, and more.

The incidence of depression in young people has increased not only in this country, but all over the world. This is not simply because we notice it more, or because therapists diagnose it more, or because we live in a time when people are eager to find psychiatric illness where we used to see only the quite ordinary problems of growing up. The increase is provably real, and it has been accompanied, in some teenage populations, by an increase in suicide rates.

Suicide, of course, remains rare. Only a small minority of depressed teenagers actually try to kill themselves. But depression has lasting effects anyway. We have learned that people who are depressed as adolescents are much more likely to grow into adults who are depressed, and that frequent episodes of depression may even change the brain's chemistry, in some sense "scarring" it, in a way that leads to a lifetime of struggle with the illness. Furthermore, depression interferes with normal teenage social development and maturation in ways that can have permanent consequences in adulthood. Good adolescent health care demands that we look for depression in young people, diagnose it correctly, and treat it aggressively when it occurs.

Until recently, the only treatment for depression was psychological, and psychological treatments, especially for milder cases of the illness, are still widely used and highly effective. These treatments are undertaken by a number of different professionals including psychiatrists, psychologists, social workers, and other "talk therapists." In addition, since the 1960s, there have been drugs that help relieve the symptoms of depression. The latest generation of these antidepressants includes a group of medicines that have few side effects and very good results in treating major depression. These are the selective serotonin reuptake inhibitors (SSRIs) and other classes of similar medicines—of which Prozac is the most famous—that are now among the most commonly prescribed drugs in the United States. These medicines have revolutionized the treatment of this disease, so much so that drug therapy is now considered by almost all professionals as the first-line treatment for severe cases of major depression.

Despite the success of these drugs, depression in teenagers remains an illness difficult to diagnose and sometimes frustratingly resistant to treatment. Drugs help, but drugs in combination with psychotherapy almost always works better. Studies have shown that the drugs work best when prescribed and monitored by specialists, and the medical specialists in treating depression are psychiatrists. This is not to minimize the importance of other professionals in treating depression. In fact, most youngsters will be seen most often not by psychiatrists but by psychologists, social workers, school counselors, and others, and their contribution to the treatment of depression is essential. Under the best of circumstances, these professionals work together as a team to provide the most effective treatment.

In this book you'll read the words of kids who have themselves been depressed, which will help parents understand what adolescent depression feels like and show depressed teenagers that they are not alone. But this book is not a substitute for competent medical care. Depression cannot be treated or relieved by reading a book about it and then applying "good advice," however well informed or well intentioned such advice might be. Instead we intend to explain what is scientifically known about the illness, help you recognize it when it occurs, and guide you, armed with reliable scientific information, toward the best possible treatment.

UNDERSTANDING
TEENAGE
DEPRESSION

1

Teenage Depression:
More Common Today Than Ever

Some estimates are that as many as 8 percent of adolescents suffer from depression at some time during any one-year period, making it much more common than, for example, eating disorders, which seem to get more attention as a source of adolescent misery. This book will tell you what you need to know about depression—whether you are the teenager suffering from it, or the parent who loves a depressed teenager.

Even among psychiatrists and other mental health care professionals, the extent of the disability caused by depression is vastly underestimated. The World Health Organization has found that major depression is the single greatest cause of disability in the world—more than twice as many people are disabled by depression as by the second leading cause of disability, iron-deficiency anemia. Other diseases and disorders may get more press or more research money, or more sympathy and concern from a well-meaning public, but major depression causes more long-term human misery than any other single disease.

When I was a resident in psychiatry, we believed that true depression was rare among teenagers, or that insofar as it existed, it was just a normal phase of adolescent development with no lasting consequences. It didn't take long after I began treating troubled kids to see that this couldn't possibly be true. Research over recent decades has confirmed my impression. These beliefs, if anyone still holds them, are false and dangerous. In fact, early onset depression is not normal, and can predict numerous unhappy life events for youngsters, including school failure, teenage pregnancy, and suicide attempts.

Although depression is today increasingly common, it is among the oldest diseases recorded in the history of medicine. As early as the fourth century, the symptoms of "melancholia" were well known and attributed to an excess of "black bile." In other words, depression was first thought of as an exclusively physical illness—the loss of appetite, sleeplessness, irritability, and general despondency of depression were believed to have a physical, not a psychological, cause. It wasn't until the nineteenth century—when the term depression was invented to substitute for melancholia—that a psychological understanding of the illness began to develop. Eventually this psychological explanation of depression would become the only one, although today it no longer is. We now know that depression has both psychological and physical symptoms, and that both psychological and medical treatments can help to alleviate them.

DEPRESSION IS A DISEASE

Depression—that is, the illness that is often called "clinical depression"—is not the same as a bad mood, or a feeling of unhappiness. It is a disease. Although there are some theories about it, no one knows exactly what causes depression in teenagers (or in anyone else, for that matter), but we do know that it is not caused by poor parenting, and that it cannot be cured by good parenting. Nor is it caused by the victim of the disease, something that is for some people all too easy to conclude. A "change in attitude" or a willingness on the part of the youngster to "straighten up and fly right" will not relieve the terrible symptoms of depression. It is a disease that requires the attention of experienced professionals, using both medical and psychological treatments, methods scientifically established as valuable in relieving the symptoms of depression and allowing a teenager to lead a normal life. These techniques are complex, time-consuming, and sometimes expensive, and they require not only the conscientious work of medical professionals but considerable cooperation from the teenager being treated, as well as the dedicated attention of the people who love her. Nor are they 100 percent effective 100 percent of the time. But they do work, and when they do they provide relief that many patients describe with the most thankful phrases: "I've been given back my life, I'm myself again" or similar words are often heard when a youngster's depression begins to lift.

PSYCHIATRIC TREATMENT THAT SAVES LIVES

Phil was a 19-year-old sophomore at a Big Ten school. He was a serious athlete—an almost Olympic-caliber ice hockey player—and a top-notch student as well, majoring in chemistry. He had had some problems during early adolescence—for a brief period he was hanging out with a group of daily marijuana smokers—but certainly no serious psychiatric illness. In any case, his parents, one of whom had had a depressive episode, were very much invested in his academic and athletic success and minimized any emotional complaints, which they viewed as a sign of weakness.

No sooner had hockey practice begun, however, than Phil had a serious falling out with one of his teammates, whose ex-girlfriend he had begun to date. This boy turned other players against him, and Phil found himself excluded from the social life of the team, essentially shunned. Gradually he became isolated from his other friends as well and began having trouble concentrating on his studies. His grades suffered. He started drinking heavily, and one night he told one of his friends that he was thinking of jumping off the roof of a building, if only he had the guts to do it. This friend called Phil's parents, his parents called me, and I urged them to either hospital-ize him there or bring him home. His father flew to the Midwest to get him, and we hospitalized him immediately upon his arrival home.

Phil's own attitude was that hospitalization wouldn't help, but, feeling despairing or numb, he put up no resistance to the plan. His time in the hospital began with the quick establishment of an anti-depressant medicine regimen, along with individual and group psy-chotherapy. His family also needed therapy and education to help them recognize that Phil suffered from a real illness, not from moral weakness.

After two weeks in the hospital and now well established on a drug regimen, Phil came home and worked for several months, then returned to school. Although he never went back to playing hockey, he has done well in college, and has continued his medication with almost complete relief from symptoms. The treatment he received in the psychiatric hospital quite literally saved his life.

That the incidence of depression is increasing has been shown in many studies all over the world—it's not just a case of our noticing it more than we used to, or becoming more sensitive to its presence. Other psychiatric disorders—bipolar illness, panic disorder, pho-bias—do not show similar increases. At the same time, suicide among all teenagers in the past fifteen years has grown by almost 25 percent, and among certain groups the rise is even higher. For exam-ple, black male adolescents, for reasons that are unclear, have seen a startling 146 percent increase in suicides in the same period. To the extent that these larger numbers are caused by an increase in the rate of depression, major depression must be considered a potentially fatal illness.

How do we know that there are more depressed teenagers now than ever before? Researching the epidemiology of psychiatric illnesses presents many problems. First, there must be general agreement on exactly what constitutes depression (discussed in more detail in chapter 2). Second, it is difficult to identify those people who are suffering from depression but who have never gone to a doctor for it, or to find the many people who seek treatment not from psychiatrists but from other health care professionals. Finally, women and affluent people are much more likely to seek treatment from psychiatrists than anyone else, and you don't get a complete picture of the problem by looking only at them. However, these obstacles have been overcome recently with large-scale community-based population studies made possible by improvements in diagnostic methods for psychiatric disorders. These community-based studies are *naturalistic*—that is, they are carried out in the community on an existing population rather than in a medical setting on a group specifically chosen and signed up for a study. In this case, the subjects were selected by their age: adolescence.

These large studies showed surprising results. Depression was once thought to be a disease of the middle-aged and elderly, but the lifetime prevalence rates—the percentage of people who experience an episode of depression in their lives—was much higher for younger people than for older people. In all of these studies, many more women than men suffer from depression, although there is some evidence that the gap is narrowing in recent years.

We psychiatrists were puzzled by the results, and looked hard for defects in the experimental technique that could explain them. I was seeing lots of depressed youngsters, but so what? That was the kind of practice I had chosen. But I didn't think that it could actually be proven that depression was generally increasing everywhere. Some suggested that the increase was an illusion because older people with depression tend to die earlier, so there are fewer of them. But it turns out that it is actually younger depressed people who have a slightly higher death rate (often from suicide and accidents). Maybe, some psychiatrists thought, young people with depression migrate from rural areas into cities, where the studies are conducted. But in rural areas and cities alike the studies find increases in the number of young people who are depressed. Then it was thought that maybe the criteria for what constituted depression had changed over time to include more people, and that this could explain the phenomenon. So researchers looked at the severity of criteria—hospitalization, duration of symptoms, treatment with drugs or electroconvulsive therapy—and tried to discern some difference among these groups. They couldn't find any. Then the researchers thought that maybe what used to be called "adolescent turmoil" or "adolescent rebellion" or "adolescent angst" was now being more frequently diagnosed as depression, and that this might account for a perceived increase in depression rates among youngsters. But the data gathered were derived from community samples, in which many had never had any psychiatric diagnosis or treatment, so this was unlikely to be the answer.

More objections were raised: maybe people now label as depression what used to be called just part of the human condition, maybe people report more symptoms if you ask them to report them, maybe old people don't remember that they were once depressed. No, no, and no. Each idea was carefully considered, but none could stand up as an explanation for the increased rates of depression among young people. In other words, as far as anyone can tell, the increase is real—it is not what researchers call an "artifact" of the way the studies were done, and it is not an illusion.

So what's going on here? Why is depression increasing? Genetics alone is unlikely as the sole explanation, because genetic changes don't normally occur in so short a time span. And environment alone can't be the explanation, because depression is known to be at least partly genetic—you're much more likely to get it if your parents had it. Messy and complicated though it may be, that leaves the gene-environment interaction as the only place left to look for explanations.

The inheritance of depression doesn't follow the neat Mendelian patterns you learned about in high school biology. Not everyone with parents who have been depressed suffers from depression, and not everyone with depression has parents who suffered from depression. Some scientists have theorized that there has been a gene mutation recently which happens to coincide with some environmental factor to produce more depression—that the increase is restricted to those people who carry this genetic mutation, perhaps especially among women and girls. But this is a theory that so far has resisted definitive proof.

There is overwhelming evidence that parents who have suffered from depression are more likely to have kids who suffer from the same disease—I see this often with my patients. But—and I repeat—this does not mean that parents by some action or behavior can cause depression in their kids. While a parent's episode of depression is not proof that his or her kids will have depression, studies have shown that the rates of depression in the families of depressed youngsters are higher than in the general population. You might guess that a depressed parent somehow creates an environment in which depression becomes more likely in the offspring. Family environment, after all, does influence certain kinds of psychiatric illness—substance abuse and alcoholism, for example. But when scientists try to find environmental causes for clinical depression in teenagers, they largely come up empty. In the case of clinical depression, genetics is probably somewhat more significant than environment. Some researchers believe that genetic factors may be slightly more significant for girls than for boys.

One extensive study done at Columbia University and published in the *Journal of the American Academy of Child and Adolescent Psychiatry* demonstrated a thirteen-fold increased risk of early onset major depression in the offspring of parents who had themselves suffered from early onset depression. Other studies have found increased rates of depression in the first- and second-degree relatives of adolescents who suffer from depression. (First-degree relatives are siblings and parents; second degree are uncles, aunts, and first cousins.) These correlations appear to exist only for major depression—neither other mood disorders nor other psychiatric illnesses follow the same pattern. All this suggests strongly that depression is an inherited disorder, or at least that genetic factors play a large role in the disease.

The mothers of depressed teenagers have particularly high rates of depression; there is less of a correlation with fathers' rates. Among depressed mothers, those who have depressed children typically have had an earlier age of onset than those who do not have depressed children. The closer the relative of the depressed youngster, the more likely that relative is to suffer from depression. First-degree relatives are as much as five times more likely to be depressed than more distant relatives. Between one-half and three-quarters of depressed kids have mothers who suffer from the same illness.

It is early onset depression—under age 16—that correlates most closely with parental depression. The incidence of onsets of depression after age 16 is more or less the same whether the parents are depressed or not.

So, on a practical level, what can we conclude from these statistical findings? If a mother has been depressed herself, and if her depression came on in childhood or early adolescence, she is more likely than other mothers to have teenagers who are depressed. But not all mothers who fit this description will have depressed teenagers. In fact, most won't—most teenagers do not become depressed, even most teenage offspring of this group of "most likely to have depressed teenagers" mothers. But a consideration of genetic tendencies in disease—whether the disease is Tay-Sachs, breast cancer, or depression—may prove useful, even if at present it only serves to alert parents to the possibility of the problem in their children.

Children of depressed parents, particularly those of depressed parents younger than 30, are at higher risk than others. With these youngsters in particular, then, parents should be aware that a professional evaluation of behavioral symptoms may be useful. Interestingly, we have learned that parents who take their kids for evaluation are often also looking for an evaluation for themselves—and this may be a good idea. In addition to suffering more from depression, the children of depressed parents are likely to have more emotional, social, and school problems, and suffer more head injuries and other accidents.

DEPRESSION ACROSS THE GENERATIONS

Depression, like many other diseases, can be inherited, and sometimes the genetic component is painfully obvious. It can be extremely troublesome to a child to feel that she has inherited some "craziness" from a parent. Nickie's father had suffered from severe depression all his life, episodes that were complicated by panic attacks so severe that he was at times afraid to leave the house. He died unexpectedly after a routine medical test procedure. Nickie, his only daughter (she has four older brothers), was 17, a senior in high school. She was of course devastated by her father's death, but she seemed to be mourning normally and gradually recovering. Then, six months into her freshman year at college, she developed a depression that looked almost exactly like her father's, even to the extent that it was accompanied by anxiety so severe that it led to panic attacks. But for very good and obvious reasons, she didn't want to be like her father—his deterioration had been all too evident to her throughout her childhood. When I suggested a course of medicine, she was aggressively opposed to the idea. "I can do this myself. I'm not sick like Dad was." The idea that she might be suffering in the same way her father had was actually preventing her from getting the treatment she needed. It took a long time to convince her that medicine would help her focus, eliminate panic, and let her be herself again.

Often it is only when I bring in a parent to discuss a child's depression that I learn that the parent is depressed too. Rosemary was a senior in high school, extremely accomplished as a musician—she played the cello well enough to play with three adults in an amateur chamber music quartet—and a brilliant math student as well. She was a middle child with accomplished siblings and parents who were highly successful academics. She was extremely attached to her family, so much so that any kind of separation from them was painful—when they were out of her sight, she was convinced they would meet with some terrible accident and die. She had had some therapy for depression and anxiety, but every time a doctor suggested that medicine might help her, she had always successfully talked both herself and the doctor out of it. Her family was against it too—they believed that taking a psychiatric medicine proved you were "crazy," and they wanted no part of it. Rosemary was still in therapy with a psychologist when she came back to see me after graduating from high school.

What she said caught me by surprise, though looking back on it perhaps it shouldn't have. "My mother has been recently diagnosed with depression, but she thinks she has probably been depressed for years. Now she's seeing a psychiatrist and she's taking an antidepressant," she explained. "She really seems much calmer, and then we found out that my older sister has been on medication for panic attacks since she started law school. This sounds silly, but I'd like to try medication because they think I'd be much better on it. . . . Maybe it's time for me to be a different person."

We decided that Rosemary should try the same medication her mother and sister had responded to. It had the same beneficial effect for her as it had for them—she did, in some sense, become quite different (though not a different person). She stopped worrying about her family dying whenever she was separated from them and felt hopeful about the future, secure, and comfortable. The genetic component of depression was never so clear: two sisters and their mother, all depressed, all responded to antidepressants. It doesn't always work this way, but when it does, it can be truly astonishing.

How about the environment? There are clearly observable differences between the environment of people born after World War II and that of those born before. In the United States and western Europe, those born after World War II generally grew up more physically healthy and economically secure than their parents. Yet not only are their rates of depression higher, but their rates of alcoholism, substance abuse, and suicide are too. Some have suggested that the epidemic of teenage drug use that began in the late 1960s may be one cause, since the groups in which depression has increased are the same groups among whom increased drug use was prevalent. But even though these two phenomena occurred at the same time, there is no definitive proof they are related. Various other environmental and social changes have been suggested as a cause: demographic changes, increased urbanization, greater geographic mobility with a loss of extended family ties, changes in family structure, changes in the roles of women (especially their increased presence in the workforce), changes in the kinds of jobs that men and women do, and a general loosening of strict standards of social behavior with a corresponding increase in individual isolation. In some particular locations, there are specific events that might help to explain an increase in depression—the wars in Lebanon in the 1970s, for example, may be part of the reason for an increase in rates of depression there at that time.

It's easy to think of environmental changes like these, but scientists have found it much harder to prove they have anything to do with depression. But it can be said now with certainty that major depression occurs just about everywhere, and that younger people everywhere are increasingly at risk. As many as one-third of young women and one-fifth of young men have been depressed at some time in their lives, and the rates are growing. Depression among teenagers is a significant public health problem.

The average age of onset of depression in adolescents is about 15, but it is not uncommon in kids from ages 10 to 14. After age 15 or so, girls are about twice as likely as boys to be depressed, and this sex difference persists until about age 55, when the number of men and women who suffer starts to be about the same. Why? No one knows for sure, but there is some evidence that fluctuations in estrogen levels during the menstrual cycle have something to do with it—the rates for women rise at roughly the age when menstruation begins, and decline when menopause starts. You might guess that women tend to report more depression—they ruminate more, express their feelings more openly, and appear depressed while men successfully hide their depression, thinking it "unmanly" to reveal such feelings. But studies have shown that this is not true, and that it can't be the explanation for men's observed lower rates of depression. There is some evidence that men forget past depression more than women, and that this may account for the statistics that show a lower lifetime rate for men. Some believe that men may more frequently medicate themselves for depression with alcohol or other drugs. Another theory holds that adolescent girls are more dependent on social relationships than boys, and therefore more sensitive to the loss of such relationships. This might increase stress for girls and lead to higher rates of depression. Some feel that girls think more about interpersonal stress instead of using denial, and that this may increase vulnerability. Yet none of the information we have about sex differences in depression helps to explain the increase in the prevalence of the disease in recent decades. This remains a mystery.

Gender doesn't seem to affect the duration of depressive episodes—girls and boys suffer for more or less the same period of time. Suicidal behavior, however, does often indicate that the depression will be longer lasting.

Although depression on average begins at 15, the "hazard rate" (the actuarial likelihood of becoming depressed at a given age) actually increases each year through the age of 19. Only one factor consistently predicts earlier onset: being a girl. No one has been able to establish a link between early onset and any of the other factors associated with depression—having other psychiatric disorders, a history of suicide attempts, and so on.

An episode of depression usually lasts about six to eight months. Kids who get depressed often grow into adults who get depressed—about two to three times as often as people who were not depressed as teenagers. There is even some evidence, which we'll discuss later in this chapter, that untreated depression in teenagers can lead to more—and more severe—episodes of depression in adulthood.

IN THEIR OWN WORDS: RECURRENT DEPRESSION

I experienced a "major depressive episode" from May to August of 1998. One of the things I was struggling with was the idea that my depression is recurrent. Prior to this episode, I had been feeling relatively stable for almost a year. The sense of failure I felt in having it come back was crushing, and no doubt contributed to making this new episode of depression worse.

—Anna, age 15

Depression is a recurrent disease—if a youngster has had it once, she's likely to have it again. It is difficult to know which depressed kids are likely to have recurrences, but the problem has been studied, and certain predictions can be made. Girls may have more frequent recurrences than boys. Where depression is severe and of longer duration, recurrence is more likely. On the other hand, the age of onset seems to bear little relationship to whether or not the depression will occur again. In any case, about 5 percent of kids with depression will relapse within six months, up to a quarter of them within a year, and more than a third will suffer another episode within two years. Of course, that leaves a majority who have depression once and don't suffer another episode for many years, if ever. Still, anyone who has suffered from depression must face the strong possibility that the disease will strike again.

The Importance of Medication

The new antidepressants can be remarkably effective. Some kids start on one of them and begin to feel better within weeks. The problem is that since they feel so much better, they decide they don't need medicine anymore. Often families encourage them to stop— the pills don't have too many side effects, but why put up with even minor side effects if you don't have to? There are risks involved in taking any medicine, so since you're better now, why take even a small risk? Why take a medicine when you're feeling fine? And taking pills is unnatural, isn't it? Left unspoken is the feeling that taking medicine reminds you that you're sick—proves it, in fact.

Stopping a medicine too early is an invitation to a recurrence. Richard was a high school sophomore who was a talented classical guitarist, outgoing, popular, smart, and a little rebellious. He had a family history of depression; in fact, his mother was taking Zoloft. He argued a lot with his father, mostly over who had control over what he did or didn't do. But then rather suddenly everything started going downhill—he refused music lessons, and instead sat on his bed idly strumming his guitar. He started hanging out with the wrong kids and using marijuana every day.

It was pretty clear to me after interviewing Richard that the marijuana was self-medication for the disease he was really suffering from: depression. But he and his father were totally opposed to the idea of antidepressants. Richard also wanted nothing to do with individual treatment, but agreed to go with his parents for family therapy and attend a group for adolescent substance abusers. Unfortunately, he stopped both forms of treatment within a month.

Toward the end of his sophomore year, his parents again brought him to see me. This time his depressive symptoms had rendered him almost nonfunctional. He had stopped going to school entirely. I considered hospitalization, but they decided against it because he was willing to start medication, and both parents were supportive of the plan to have individual, group, and family treatment. With these interventions, he improved dramatically within six weeks. By the fall, he was himself again and doing well. So well, in fact, that in October he decided he didn't need the medicine anymore. The medicine, he felt, was his parents' idea in the first place anyway, and now that he was better, what was the point of taking it? He wasn't doing drugs now, he was doing well in school, so he didn't need what he picturesquely referred to as "crazy pills" to keep him on track. So he stopped taking them.

By the following spring, Richard was depressed and morose and was smoking marijuana, drinking, and staying out late with the wrong crowd—exactly the problems that had brought him into my office in the first place. This time, he needed hospitalization—now both for depression and drug rehabilitation. But he learned his lesson. After his hospitalization he continued taking his medicine regularly—"crazy pills" or not—and continues to do well.

FURTHER RISKS IN DEPRESSION

Suicide is the risk in depression most often talked about, and it is obviously the most serious. (We'll discuss suicide at length in chapter 4.) Depression holds other risks as well for teenagers—substance abuse and cigarette smoking among them. The assumption that kids are using drugs for thrills and cigarettes because they consider smoking sophisticated may not always be correct. In fact, some studies suggest that cigarette smoking may help to alleviate the symptoms of depression—that is, that teens (and others) are actually medicating themselves for depression with nicotine. Other studies show that youngsters suffering from depression are more likely to succumb to the peer pressures that influence taking up the habit. The association of smoking and depression may be even more marked in teenage girls than boys. The dangers of using tobacco and drugs are well known and need no discussion here, but if they are being used as a defense against depression, or if being depressed is a reason for taking up smoking, then treating the depression is that much more important. Now, no one should conclude from this that all teenage smoking and drug abuse is itself a sure sign of depression, because it is not. But for some teenagers, getting relief from depression may actually make smoking and drug use less attractive.

Pete Harnisch, the Cincinnati Reds pitcher, attributes his severe episode of major depression to having stopped using chewing tobacco. It is possible that Harnisch was using tobacco to keep his depression under control, and that stopping it actually did initiate his plunge into severe illness. Obviously this does not happen to everyone—most people who quit using tobacco don't immediately become ill with major depression. Yet it is clearly another factor to consider in trying to understand and treat this disease.

A parent who has suffered from depression knows what it feels like, but one who hasn't may not fully understand the pain experienced by a teenager undergoing this trial. Everyone has experienced life events that have made them feel depressed. We lose a job, a friend dies, a financial setback changes our standard of living. These things, and a million others, can make a person feel sad or blue. However, even though we might feel thoroughly miserable right now, we know that somehow the feeling will pass, that things will get better, that everything will turn out all right in the end, and that we'll come back to feeling good again. And after a time, we do. We feel like our old selves, as we knew we would. Because you have had experiences like this, you may think you can imagine how a depressed person must feel. But true clinical depression isn't just being in a bad or irritable mood, or feeling blue, or sensing ordinary human sadness about an unhappy or unlucky event. It is qualitatively different from this common experience, and much worse.

IN THEIR OWN WORDS:
WHAT DOES IT FEEL LIKE?

I was sixteen and sitting in my room, crying uncontrollably. I tried to think what was making me so sad, but I didn't know. I just didn't feel *right*, but I didn't know why I was so sad. That's the worst part about it—crying and feeling like your world is ending but not knowing what is causing you to ache.

All I wanted was to be "normal." To cry when "normal" people cry and be happy when "normal" people are happy. I tricked a lot of people. My friends had no idea, because on the outside I was a regular high school girl, but on the inside I was falling apart. I was too embarrassed to tell them: "I cry and feel sad all the time and I don't know why."

It wasn't easy to hide it from my parents and sisters. They'd ask what was wrong and the instant response was, "Nothing." Don't you understand? I don't know what's wrong! I don't like myself and I don't want to do anything or see anyone and I feel sad and confused and alone and helpless and I do want to snap out of this, I do! But I can't!

Then came the guilt. After all, what the hell was I whining about? I had a loving family and wonderful friends. I was a straight-A student and a varsity athlete and involved in virtually every club and extracurricular. I was just weak and selfish. There were starving children in Ethiopia for Christ's sake—they had a right to cry. Why the hell was I such a selfish wimp?

The pain and sadness were close to unbearable at times. I questioned everything—"Why am I here? What good am I? Why can't I just be happy?" I was guilty that my family worried about me. Maybe it would be better for everyone if there was no me. . . .

"I just don't think I can get through this" ran through my head every minute of every day. Whenever I hear people say that "suicide is the most selfish act of any person," I just think that they have no concept of what it's like to be depressed.

—Courtney, age 16

What happens to depressed adolescents as they grow to adulthood? Depression is usually a time-limited disease, so depressed kids almost always recover from their episodes, even if they don't get proper treatment. But adolescents who have been depressed are up to three times as likely to have further episodes of depression in adulthood. In fact, 70 percent of adolescents who have a first episode of depression will have subsequent episodes. At least one long-term study has shown that even subclinical depression—irritable moods that don't meet the diagnostic criteria for major depression—can be the precursors of more severe adult depression. Anhedonia (the inability to experience ordinary pleasure) and thoughts about death during adolescence are particularly worrisome, because they correlate highly with adult depression.

Perhaps even more significantly, there is some evidence that untreated adolescent depression can lead to more frequent and more severe episodes later in life. This is called the "kindling effect," and it is only now beginning to be studied and understood. Psychiatrists have recognized in clinical observation over many years that depression is a recurrent disease, and that the time between episodes becomes shorter as the patient gets older. We also could see that while a stressful event might precede the first episode of depression, following episodes were less likely to be dependent on such "stressors," or could be provoked by seemingly milder and milder events. In other words, depression recurs more easily with repeated episodes.

Robert Post and his colleagues at the National Institute of Mental Health have tried to find a biological model that would explain these clinical observations. If you repeatedly stimulate an animal's brain with an electrical current, you produce increasingly severe seizures even without increasing the power of the electrical charge. The repeated stimulation makes the brain more sensitive to the electrical current, and the change is permanent. Post has proposed that a similar phenomenon happens in depression: repeated episodes make the brain more and more sensitive to the stresses that provoke the illness. Researchers have theorized that there is a kind of brain damage caused by depression, a permanent alteration in the brain's neurotransmitters (see chapter 8 for a discussion of the biology of depression), making a person forever more likely to become depressed. Each episode of depression, in other words, seems to change the basic "wiring" of the brain, making it more susceptible to the next episode.

It has been shown that teenagers after a first episode of depression are more likely to have behavior problems, excessive emotional reliance on others, and more physical health problems than others. They appear to be left with psychological scars.

Although the kindling effect cannot yet be considered a scientific certainty, it does offer a possible explanation for the clinical observations about the course of depression. This has made most clinicians feel that long-term, even lifelong therapy for depression is best. Preventing relapse may mean preventing permanent changes in the brain.

In short, depression is a serious disease that must be diagnosed and treated as soon as possible. So how can you tell if a teenager is depressed? That is what we will discuss in the next chapter.

2

Diagnosis: Figuring Out If Depression Is the Problem

You now know that depression is usually a time-limited disease—an episode will last six to eight months and then end. So, you may ask, why not just tell the teenager to try to "tough it out" and let the depression go away on its own? Why bother with complicated, time-consuming, expensive treatments that don't always work perfectly anyway, when in a few months the whole thing will be gone? Several problems with this approach make it very dangerous.

First, depression is extremely painful—comparable in severity to the worst kind of physical pain. No one would ask a teenager (or anyone else for that matter) to "tough out" even ten minutes of pain from, say, filling a cavity in a tooth. Why ask a victim of depression to tough out the equally severe pain of depression for as long as eight months?

Next, not all depression goes away so conveniently. In some cases, symptoms may last for years. In others, the patient recovers somewhat between episodes, but never enough to be feeling really well. How long is it worth it to remain stoical, and what is gained by doing so? How long is too long to put up with an illness that can be treated effectively? Even more important, untreated depression is a major cause of suicide. What if your teenager decides to harm himself while you're waiting for him to pull through the episode?

Third, during the episode of depression, a kid misses out on opportunities for normal social and intellectual development, opportunities that may be difficult or impossible to reclaim later, and which may have ill effects that last a lifetime. And finally, there is good evidence that untreated depression in teenagers leads to increased episodes of depression in adulthood. I always try hard to convince kids and their parents that depression must be treated, and it must be treated every time it recurs.

In a sense, each episode of depression leaves scars that don't disappear. Even after recovery, formerly depressed kids show difficulties in relationships with their peers, parents, and siblings. One study found that excessive desire for support and approval from others and anxiety when left alone or considered abandoned increased significantly after an episode of depression had ended. In addition, the study found that adolescents increased their rate of smoking after depressive episodes. These residual effects of an episode of depression suggest that adolescent-onset depression may be even more severe than the same disease in adults.

Teenagers can be moody, as every parent knows, but every moody teenager is not suffering from depression. Most teenagers, even the ones who are really acting up, do not have clinical depression. I see lots of kids who are just being teenagers—suffering the pains of finding their place in an adult world that still seems foreign territory. They can't act like kids anymore—they know that, and they don't want to anyway—but they haven't yet figured out how to act like adults. This, naturally, leads to many unpleasant feelings: inadequacy, self-doubt, worry, sometimes something close to despair about ever being able to function successfully in the world as it is. But unpleasant as all this can be, it's nothing compared to clinical depression. About 10 percent of teenagers suffer from depressed mood without actually being clinically depressed. But among those clinically depressed, almost 100 percent suffer from persistent despondency.

Only physicians and other mental health professionals can definitively diagnose clinical depression (the diagnosis is much simpler in severe cases than in mild cases), but parents need to know when it's time to seek help—even if they're not sure depression is the problem. It is difficult to distinguish the normal mood variations and emotional storms of adolescence from a real disease, and parents can be of considerable help in figuring it out.

Kids may express their depression with certain kinds of bad behavior that can be either a manifestation of the illness itself or a way of trying to alleviate its terrible symptoms. These include having temper tantrums, cutting school and failing courses, running away from home, stealing, using drugs, engaging in promiscuous sexual behavior, and other kinds of delinquency. These kinds of misbehavior are not always indicative of depression, but in getting to the bottom of the problem, I always look for depression as one important possibility.

WHAT'S A DISEASE, WHAT ISN'T, AND HOW DO YOU TELL THE DIFFERENCE?

Depression has no known single cause. There's no germ, no blood test, no single finding in a physical examination that will tell you that depression is definitely the problem. Instead, we rely on a constellation of observed and reported symptoms, which, taken together and properly weighted, result in an accurate diagnosis. These criteria are not vague or subjective: psychiatric researchers have worked very hard at making them as specific and objective as possible. I may informally say to a parent or a colleague, "She seems depressed to me," but I'm basing the statement on specific observations widely agreed upon by the profession.

In this sense, psychiatric diagnosis is no different from diagnosis in any other field of medicine. "Disease" is a human invention, not a phenomenon of nature. A cold, for example, is caused by a rhinovirus, and a virus is, of course, a phenomenon of nature, existing out there apart from us. But the virus is not a cold. A "cold" is an invented category used to describe what happens when that rhinovirus takes up residence inside a human body. Similarly, having a fasting blood sugar level above 140 mg/dl is not diabetes until we humans define that level of blood sugar as the disease called "diabetes." Categorizing symptoms into diseases is a method of organization and description, a guide to selecting treatments (and doing reliable research), and a method of predicting the outcome for the person involved. This can be done effectively even when the actual cause of a disease is unknown. No one knows exactly what causes diabetes, or Lou Gehrig's disease, or Alzheimer's disease, or hypertension, or hundreds of other ailments, but they can be quite accurately described from their symptoms. Based on this, treatment can be implemented, and accurate predictions about the effectiveness of that treatment and the course of the disease can be made.

Some diseases are easier to diagnose—categorize—than others. If a doctor suspects a person has strep throat, for example, there is a simple test that gives a definitive answer: you take a throat swab, and culture it. If what grows in the petri dish is the streptococcus bacterium, then a definitive diagnosis of strep throat is made. With other diseases, there are no simple lab tests, or no tests at all. In these cases, the diagnosis is arrived at by observing symptoms and eliminating other possible causes for them. This is true of many physical illnesses, and of virtually all psychiatric illnesses.

A head cold has familiar symptoms—your nose is running, you have a headache, you're coughing and sneezing. There are of course mild and severe colds, and many varieties of viruses that cause them. Sometimes a person has a cough but nothing else. Sometimes the cough is accompanied by chest pain, sometimes it isn't. Some people get headaches, some don't. Aspirin helps some people feel better. Others need cough medicine. Some people only feel better if they stay in bed. So, while everyone knows more or less what a cold looks like, there are many causes, plenty of variations in symptoms from one person to the next, and a variety of different ways to treat those symptoms. All this is true of brain disorders as well.

ARE YOU DEPRESSED, OR JUST SAD?

Lots of people feel sad from time to time—life gives us all ample reason for this, and that a teenager feels sad is not by itself a reason to conclude he suffers from the psychiatric illness called depression. A psychiatrist has to go considerably beyond this to establish a diagnosis.

A Psychiatric Interview

A psychiatric interview is a conversation, but it's not like a conversation you have with a friend. It respects few of the ordinary rules of social discourse. Instead, it is designed to make a diagnosis—that is, find out "where it hurts"—and then develop a realistic plan for treatment.

Cynthia was acting so unlike herself that one of her friends told the peer counselor at the high school about her. The friend reported that Cynthia seemed always in some kind of despair these days about her life and her future. She was unable to enjoy the things she was usually enthusiastic about, and appeared down and discouraged, but when asked what was getting her down she was unable to say. When Cynthia finally said something about "not wanting to be here anymore" her friends really got scared. That's when they went to the high school's peer counselor and told her something was seriously wrong. The peer counselor—quite correctly—sent Cynthia to the emergency room for evaluation. I came into the room, and she was sitting on a gurney, looking upset and tearful. Her parents and one of her friends were there, too. I introduced myself, "I'm Dr. Empfield, and I'm the psychiatrist." I asked the others to leave so that Cynthia and I could talk in private. The teenager seemed somewhat relieved to be in this setting with someone to listen to her. After a discussion of possible medical problems, which revealed nothing of interest, this is the discussion that ensued.

Dr. Empfield: Can you tell me what's been going on?

I skip the small talk so Cynthia knows I'm concerned about what is really troubling her.

Cynthia: Laura thought I needed to see someone.

Dr. Empfield: All I know is that your friends are worried about you. Do you think they're right to be worried?

Cynthia silently looks down at her feet.

Dr. Empfield: Do you think that Laura was right? That you need to see someone?

Cynthia: Yeah, I guess so.

Dr. Empfield: I think so too. I mean, I think they're right to be concerned. Laura told me that you had planned to go away for the weekend, but that now you don't want to. Can you tell me why? Has something changed recently?

Cynthia: No, nothing's different. I just didn't feel like going away for the weekend.

Dr. Empfield: What was supposed to happen during the weekend?

Cynthia: It's just some regional Amnesty International thing. It wasn't that important, and I just didn't feel like going all the way up to Boston.

Dr. Empfield: Were you sad or upset about something?

Cynthia: No . . . well . . . I don't know.

Dr. Empfield: Sometimes you can just lose interest in things without really feeling sad. Does that happen sometimes?

Silence.

Dr. Empfield: Has anything happened that made you feel sad?

Cynthia: I'm fighting with my mother all the time. I don't know why.

Dr. Empfield: So that's one thing that's been happening. Have you been sleeping all right?

Cynthia: Not really, I have to fall asleep in front of the TV. We fight about that too.

Dr. Empfield: How about your appetite?

Cynthia: Oh, it's all right.

Dr. Empfield: How are your grades?

Cynthia: Not so hot. Usually I do OK, but lately, I don't know . . .

Dr. Empfield: I know you like rock climbing—and you play field hockey, don't you?

Cynthia: I quit the team. It stopped being fun a while ago. I haven't been doing much climbing either. I don't feel like it lately.

Dr. Empfield: When do you think you started feeling so bad?

Cynthia: A couple of months ago, maybe. I really didn't notice it—people started telling me. In fact, everyone's kind of annoying me about it. I don't want to spend any time with them.

Dr. Empfield: Do you feel anxious, like something bad might happen?

Cynthia: Sometimes. Not all the time.

Dr. Empfield: What makes you anxious?

Cynthia: Bad grades. If I've cut class and my mother's going to find out about it.

Dr. Empfield: Do you use marijuana?

Cynthia: I've tried it, but I don't like it.

Dr. Empfield: Do you drink alcohol?

Cynthia: Only on weekends.

These last answers should not be taken as a "no." Usually such answers mean that the youngster is actively using drugs and alcohol. Even the most adamant denials often turn out to be dishonest, and mild admissions can mean regular use. If a kid says, "I've been drinking more lately," then you may really have something to be concerned about.

Thus we have a girl whose grades have been falling, who has abandoned her usual friends. She's fighting with her parents, losing interest in studying, and doesn't like her favorite activities anymore. I am trying to establish a rapport, not criticizing any of this. But I'm getting the picture. School is important, and when you start failing, it means trouble. When she decides she doesn't want to go away this weekend, that's troublesome too. I have to start thinking about whether she has some plan to hurt herself.

Dr. Empfield: Do you feel sad sometimes?

Cynthia: Last week I was driving to school and I just started crying for no reason.

Dr. Empfield: Have you told anyone about it?

Cynthia: No, they'd just bring me to a place like this. I'm not crazy, you know.

Dr. Empfield: No, you're not. But have you ever felt that things just aren't worth it, and that you'd just as soon not be here?

Cynthia: Everyone feels like that sometimes.

Dr. Empfield: That's true, but sometimes the feelings are stronger than at other times. Do you have thoughts that really stay with you about harming yourself?

Cynthia: No.

Dr. Empfield: Well, it's not too unusual to have such thoughts. It's hard to figure out a way out of certain situations. It sounds like you had people you could talk to, but you don't talk to them anymore. What I'm concerned about is that maybe you're thinking that this weekend you want to stop your pain by hurting yourself in some way. And maybe that's why you canceled your trip.

Cynthia: No, no.

Dr. Empfield: Have you ever done anything like that—tried to harm yourself?

Cynthia: A long time ago. I took six aspirins. I just felt sick and went to bed.

Dr. Empfield: What made you do that?

Cynthia: It was a fight with my mother.

Now I'm starting to see that Cynthia can be impulsive. If she took the aspirin last week, it's more troublesome than if it were last year. But by this time, it is obvious that Cynthia is depressed. Her depression has been going on for some months. Now the only question is whether she is acutely ill and needs to be hospitalized or whether she can be treated as an outpatient.

Dr. Empfield: Let's get back to this weekend. What made you decide not to go with your friends?

Cynthia: I just didn't feel like it.

Dr. Empfield: I'm going to ask you a question that may make you feel uncomfortable, but I want you to try to answer it as honestly as you can. Did you have any kind of plan to harm yourself?

Cynthia (after some time in silence): Well, my mother has pain pills for her back. I know where she keeps them. I've thought about it before, but I wouldn't take them.

If she had said that there was a gun in the house, I would immediately hospitalize the teenager. If she had come to school drunk, or been in a car accident recently, that would also be reason for immediate hospitalization. But that's not the case here.

Dr. Empfield: Why wouldn't you?

Cynthia: I know it would hurt my parents. And my friends.

This is reassuring. She has some ideas about why she shouldn't hurt herself, and how doing so would affect the people she cares about.

Dr. Empfield: Do you think you need to be in a hospital to be safe?

Cynthia: No, just let me go home, I'm fine.

Dr. Empfield: Well, what are you going to do this weekend—since you've canceled your other plans?

Cynthia: Just hang out.

Dr. Empfield: Well, that's not a good plan. If you're not going to be in the hospital, we have to make some plans for this weekend, and for seeing a doctor the first thing next week. You have a depression—that's actually not such an uncommon problem. We can even treat it, which is good news. You don't have to keep feeling this bad. I know it's scary, but it's a good thing that you came here today. Now we have to figure out what we're going to do next. "Just hanging out" isn't good enough for this weekend.

"Just hanging out" is an invitation to trouble. Cynthia needs a structured plan for the weekend, with someone monitoring her, but I can work this out with her and her parents, using on-call staff if I have to. Often this is a relief to a kid—she realizes that she's not just bad, and that there may be reasons for the way she feels, and some hope for relief from feeling that way. After a discussion like this, I know what the problem is, and I can see a way to make some plans for Cynthia to get the treatment she needs.

The Hurdles in an Interview

With teenagers, there are hurdles in an interview that have to be overcome. Kids can be angry with adults, or even just reluctant to talk on the general principle that adults are as a group untrustworthy. Often, I can see a youngster sizing me up when he first meets me, trying to determine whether I am a potential ally or just another adult to be wary of. On the other hand, there can be a sense of relief when a kid sees that you can be a possible advocate, and with that realization the reluctance to discuss problems can begin to disappear.

A psychiatric interview with a teenager is a very different proposition from an interview with an adult. While some kids are eager to talk, at least as many are initially determined to remain silent and uncooperative. The ordinary anger and distrust of adults can be particularly severe when it is a "doctor for crazy people" that they are now faced with. I work hard to gain the trust that will result in a teenager revealing her thoughts and feelings in an honest way that will help lead to a successful outcome. I'm empathic, I refrain from making judgments, I accept what the teenager brings to the interview. A sense of humor is essential, and it is especially important for the therapist to be able to laugh at herself. Many teenagers view going to a psychiatrist or any other mental health professional as a defeat or a humiliation, so it's my job to help the youngster move beyond these feelings toward cooperation. This requires patience and understanding of a kind qualitatively different from what would be necessary and appropriate with most adult patients. None of this comes naturally, at least not at first. Successful interviewing, especially with teenagers, depends both on techniques that can be learned and on experience.

The DSM

Like other medical specialties, psychiatry has a manual of diagnosis that lays out in great detail the definitions of the illnesses the specialty concerns itself with. It is called the *Diagnostic and Statistical Manual of Mental Disorders* (DSM), and it is presently in its fourth edition (DSM-IV). It is more or less constantly being updated as knowledge improves, and from time to time revised editions are published.

For each disorder, the DSM lists diagnostic criteria, the subtypes of each disease, guidelines for recording the appropriate name and numerical code (on an insurance form, for example), associated laboratory and physical exam findings, specific cultural, age, or gender features of the illness, its prevalence, its course, its family patterns, and its differential diagnosis. This last category, differential diagnosis, is the most important, because this is the process by which a psychiatrist distinguishes a disease from the limited number of other diseases that it may resemble. This is the way, in other words, that a psychiatrist arrives at a diagnosis.

MEDICAL ILLNESS AND PSYCHIATRIC ILLNESS

One of the things that makes psychiatric diagnosis so difficult is that many medical illnesses can begin with psychiatric symptoms, and these must be eliminated from consideration before a purely psychiatric diagnosis can be made. If the thyroid gland, for example, begins to malfunction by producing too much or too little thyroid hormone, these chemical changes in the body can produce depression, even before there are any overt physical symptoms of thyroid disease.

The most common physical causes of depression are the use of drugs (including both illegal drugs and the proper use of prescribed medicines), endocrine system malfunctions, and diseases of the central nervous system such as multiple sclerosis. Symptoms of depression can also be present in those with heart disease, Alzheimer's disease, cancer, and lupus, though these diseases are extremely rare among teenagers. In certain parts of the country Lyme disease is a problem among adolescents, and this infection, if it is untreated, can also lead to depression. Other likely physical causes for depression among adolescents are head injury, mononucleosis, chronic fatigue syndrome, and hepatitis in its various forms.

Mononucleosis is a common disease of adolescence with a variable course—it can have mild symptoms and last for only a few weeks, or it can cause severe liver dysfunction and last for years. But it often begins with a feeling of lassitude and depression, and it isn't all that easy to diagnose. It requires a blood test, which may come back negative in the early stages of the disease, and only come back positive with a later test. Since mono is typically a disease of adolescents and young adults, it is important to rule it out.

Chronic fatigue syndrome is still a somewhat mysterious disease, probably caused by the Epstein-Barr virus that is also involved in certain kinds of hepatitis. Its most vivid symptom—fatigue that begins abruptly and lasts for months—looks a lot like depression, so much so, in fact, that some physicians have tried, with mixed success, using antidepressants to treat it.

At least a half-dozen different kinds of viruses cause hepatitis, but they all cause similar symptoms: loss of appetite, malaise, nausea, vomiting, fever. And they can cause mental symptoms ranging from slight depression to psychotic hallucinations. Hepatitis is a common disease, especially hepatitis A, and teenagers can get it just as easily as anyone else.

All of the diseases mentioned above should be ruled out as a cause of the problem before treatment for depression is undertaken, so a complete physical examination is essential. I sometimes do some physical assessment, such as taking a blood pressure reading when patients are taking medicines that can lower it, but I would normally refer a teenager to a pediatrician or internist for a complete workup.

THE DIFFERENT KINDS OF DEPRESSION

Depression is not a single disease, but a complicated and overlapping group of diseases. The different kinds of depression described below respond to different treatments, so it is important to distinguish one from another. A teenager might suffer from any one of these types, and, as we will see, might even suffer from more than one at the same time. Psychiatrists and other experts have classified these types of depression, described their symptoms, and devised treatments for them. Telling one from another is difficult, and requires the attention of an experienced clinician. You can't diagnose yourself or your teenager, but you can understand the different kinds of depression we now know about.

Major Depression

IN THEIR OWN WORDS:
SO WEAK I CAN'T GET OUT OF BED

I was permanently tired, regardless of how much sleep I got. Some days it was too much effort even to get out of bed. The thought of facing the outside world and its inhabitants was too overwhelming. It was safer to hide under my bedsheets. But I wanted to get out of bed—"Please let my legs drag me out of bed and break the chains!" —but I couldn't. Instead, I cried for acting so weak and so sad.

—Courtney, age 16

Major depression is a physical as well as a psychological disease, with physical symptoms that increase with the severity of the disorder. The DSM-IV lists loss of appetite, fatigue, slowed movements or restlessness, weight loss, excessive sleeping, and insomnia as criteria for the diagnosis of depression. Backaches, bowel disturbances, palpitations, and other physical symptoms are quite common. In some cultures, sufferers focus almost exclusively on the physical symptoms, rarely even mentioning emotional complaints. For many, however, the most overwhelming symptoms are inconsolable misery, guilt, and despair; irritability and hostility; feelings of worthlessness; hopelessness about the future; and preoccupation with thoughts of death and suicide. Time passes slowly; concentrating is difficult; ordinary emotions, even ordinary sadness or grief, are often difficult or impossible to experience.

There are certain ways in which the diagnosis can be confusing in a teenager. For example, adolescents sleep a lot. That's normal, and not in itself a sign of depression. If parents tell me that a kid is sleeping until two in the afternoon on weekends, I may sometimes remind them of their own adolescence—there's nothing especially unusual about sleeping late. Similarly, weight gain and weight loss, provided they aren't extreme and don't involve bingeing and vomiting, can be ordinary events in a teenager's life, and not a sign of illness. So when I look at the symptoms the DSM-IV lists, I always take such things into account—some physical phenomena that might be mistaken for symptoms of depression are merely symptoms of being an adolescent. In general, the "vegetative" signs— that is, the physical symptoms that often accompany depression—are less useful in diagnosing depression in adolescents than in adults. If a teenager's eating habits seem odd, or he experiences unusual weight gain or loss, that alone would not lead me to suspect depression as a cause—these things are too much a part of being an adolescent to be considered a sign of disease. At the same time, physical complaints such as stomachaches and headaches are more common in depressed adolescents than they are in depressed adults.

Assessing physical complaints, then, becomes a matter of degree and quality. While sleeping twelve hours straight is probably perfectly normal for a teenager, the experience of exhaustion that Courtney describes (see box on page 33) is something entirely different. These are the subtle differences that a psychiatrist examining an adolescent will always have in mind.

IN THEIR OWN WORDS:
PHYSICAL SYMPTOMS OF DEPRESSION

After a trip to France with my class, I started to have a lot of stomach pain. I thought it must have been something in the water in France or something that I had eaten. When I lost weight, my mother took me to the pediatrician. He ran a few tests, then referred me to a pediatric gastroenterologist. He did more blood tests and felt my stomach, but found nothing. He removed different foods from my diet: popcorn, gum, tomato sauce, spices, pizza, and anything greasy. I also tried removing dairy foods. The new diet did nothing. I started obsessing over what I ate and mentally categorized foods into "safe" and "unsafe." Eventually almost everything became "unsafe." My doctor ordered all kinds of tests—ultrasounds, a lactose intolerance test, a colonoscopy. All came back negative.

I started seeing a new gastroenterologist. The new doctor ordered more tests, more blood tests, an endoscopy, a GI series . . . all negative. By this point, with each test I was hoping that something would be positive—I would have been happy if they had found a tumor. I wanted a medicine to stop my pain. How could I be feeling so awful if there was nothing wrong? Finally, my doctor and I were talking and she asked, "When is your stomach the worst?"

"When I'm home doing nothing. I just dwell."

"You stay home all weekend?" she wanted to know.

"Yeah."

"A tenth-grader should not be sitting home all weekend. There's something wrong with that."

I felt like she was making a statement about my not having friends or something. I felt terrible and like a total loser. She said that there really wasn't anything more she could do for me, but that maybe I should think about seeing a psychiatrist. I was desperate and if therapy could help me then I would go. I suggested to my parents that I begin therapy, and they willingly took me.

Within about a month and a half of therapy, my symptoms went

away and I felt renewed, like I'd gotten myself back. What is clear
to me now is that my stomach serves as a gauge of my emotional
well-being. When I have stomach pains or digestive problems, it
usually means that too many things have built up.

—Becky, age 15

Sometimes depressed people withdraw from others, refusing
social contact, incapable of experiencing pleasure of any kind. In the
most severe cases—up to 10 percent of hospitalized teenagers in
some studies—hallucinations and delusions can occur, and this is
sometimes called "psychotic depression." One study showed that
depressed teenagers are somewhat less likely than children to have
hallucinations and phobias, and that they show more despair, weight
change, and excessive sleep patterns than do adults who suffer from
depression. But again, teenagers are different from adults: they stay
up late, sleep until noon, and gain weight in association with normal
growth. None of this should be taken as an indication that a youngster
is depressed—unless other things are going on at the same time. Anxiety can be present at the same time as the symptoms of depression,
leading to feelings of panic, fear, or restlessness. This is sometimes
informally called "restless depression" or "anxious depression."

IN THEIR OWN WORDS: WITHDRAWING FROM
THE WORLD IN GUILT, MISERY, AND DESPAIR

Why am I reacting this way to people, to the outside world? I cannot stand being awake, and when awake I can't stand being in the
street among other human beings. I do not have the energy to communicate with anyone outside myself, and as it is I grow increasingly weary of my own company.

I try to listen to the few good CDs I have with me here, but I soon grow restless and irritated at the music I have in the past so much enjoyed. Nothing seems to be right: too quiet/loud, too slow/fast, too whiny/angry/exultant/seductive, et cetera. I try to read, but then I become afraid I am missing the song. I turn the music off and then read, but I cannot stand the silence. If I recline and try neither to read nor hear the music, I promptly fall asleep—which I like, but feel guilty about indulging.

—Anna, age 15

Depression and Unhappy Events

While the symptoms of major depression usually come on gradually, over a period of days or weeks, an episode can occur suddenly, provoked by an unhappy life event or even a sudden physiological change, like withdrawal from nicotine or alcohol.

Teenagers, like everyone else, experience unhappy events, but unhappy events do not, by themselves, cause depression (see chapter 5 for a fuller discussion of this). Still, an unhappy event can be the trigger for an episode of depression in a youngster who is already vulnerable to the disease.

The pressures of school—both social and academic—are predictable triggers for depression. In fact, I can predict the times of year when I'll have the largest number of teenagers hospitalized on my ward: more teenagers arrive in the emergency room right before school starts in September and at the end of every school vacation. High school seniors get depressed right before graduation and come into the emergency room in larger numbers in late May and early June. These school events—ordinary for most kids—are too much for some adolescents prone to depression.

Sometimes the events that precipitate depression are not so ordinary. One of my patients was pregnant. Her relationship with the baby's father was not a happy one, and the pregnancy was certainly unplanned, but still she very much wanted the baby. When she had a miscarriage, she felt terribly guilty, not just saddened by the event, and wound up seriously ill with a depression for which she had to be hospitalized. Again, the sad event didn't cause the depression—but it triggered a grave episode in a vulnerable youngster.

Categories of Major Depression

Like other diseases, a case of major depression can be more or less severe. For purposes of diagnosis, psychiatrists divide the severity into three categories—mild, moderate, and severe—but of course the symptoms exist along a continuum with infinite variations from one person to another and within the same person at different times. In the most mild cases, the teenager has only minor impairments, enough to make the diagnosis but not enough to significantly interfere with daily life and functioning. In the most severe cases, the youngster may be completely unable to carry out ordinary social or school functions, even unable to feed and clothe herself or take care of ordinary personal grooming and hygiene. In categorizing the severity of a youngster's depression, the therapist will take into account the nature of the symptoms as well. Suicidal ideas or actual suicide attempts usually mean that the depression will be categorized as severe.

GINA: HEARING VOICES

During her junior year of high school, Gina became increasingly withdrawn and began skipping classes, then entire days of school. She had been an honor student, and when she began failing subjects, her parents were called in by the school. The guidance counselor suggested that Gina might be depressed, but her parents felt she was just being lazy. They began driving her to school to assure her attendance, but she spent entire days in the guidance counselor's office sleeping. One Saturday, Gina was arrested for shoplifting. The following Monday, she told a friend that she had picked out a dress to wear when she killed herself. The friend told her own mother, who informed the school, who notified Gina's parents. Gina's parents called the police, who picked her up and brought her to our emergency room. At last, Gina told our staff something she had told no one before: she had been hearing voices making derogatory comments about her and telling her to kill herself because she was "evil." Gina was immediately admitted to the hospital with a diagnosis of depression with psychotic features.

The DSM-IV is quite specific about what constitutes major depression, listing nine different symptoms: depressed mood most of the day, nearly every day; diminished pleasure in all, or almost all activities; significant weight loss or weight gain or diminished or increased appetite every day, or most days; insomnia or sleeping too much; agitation and feelings of restlessness; fatigue or loss of energy most days; excessive or inappropriate feelings of worthlessness or guilt; diminished ability to concentrate; a suicide attempt, or recurrent thoughts of death (not just fear of dying) even without a specific plan to commit suicide. It is important to remember that although thoughts of death and suicide are the most serious symptoms of depression—symptoms so serious as to constitute an emergency in many cases—nevertheless only about half of depressed adolescents have such thoughts.

A therapist will, however, weigh these symptoms differently in a teenager than in an adult. As I've said (and as any parent will recognize), increased appetite, sleeping a lot, feeling tired, and gaining weight mean something different in a teenager's life than in an adult's. Even in a kid who is truly depressed, these symptoms have less importance than others, because almost all teenagers, depressed or not, are likely to have them. At the same time, when these symptoms are accompanied by painful psychological ideas, such as staying in bed because it feels intolerable to face the world, they take on new significance.

To justify a definitive diagnosis of major depression, a psychiatrist will have to find that at least five of the nine diagnostic symptoms have been present over a two-week period, and one of the five must be either depressed mood or loss of interest or pleasure in normally pleasurable activities.

All of these symptoms can be felt by people who nevertheless are not suffering from major depression, so the manual specifies that the symptoms must be present in the absence of bereavement, in the absence of drug abuse, and, most important, in the absence of any symptoms clearly due to a general medical condition. This last point is critical, because, I emphasize here again, many other medical disorders can cause symptoms that look exactly like depression.

Dysthymia

IN THEIR OWN WORDS: DYSTHYMIA

It's taken me a long time to understand what that diagnosis means beyond the classic psychiatric lingo, "Dysthymia is a low-grade depression." In a way, I feel that downplays the experience—claiming that it is not as serious or bad as clinical depression. In my eyes, dysthymia is as bad if not worse.

—Becky, age 20

The symptoms of dysthymia are similar to major depression, but not as severe and usually longer lasting. Depressive symptoms in this disorder occur every day or most days, and in teenagers a criterion for this diagnosis is that they last for at least a year. Poor appetite, insomnia, low energy, inability to concentrate, and feelings of hopelessness are typical. In teenagers, a persistent irritability can also be a symptom. The symptoms are similar to major depression, and if they are severe enough, the diagnosis of major depression is made instead.

Dysthymia is also distinguished from major depression by its duration—it lasts longer, with patients often reporting that "I always feel like this" or "This is just the way I am." That a teenager may view this illness as a normal state of affairs makes it more difficult to diagnose. I always make a careful effort to elicit the information—the youngster may think the feeling isn't anything particularly worth mentioning. Young people who suffer from this disorder may view themselves unrealistically as incompetent or uninteresting and feel blue most of the time for periods as long as two or three years, but the symptoms become so much a part of everyday life that the teenager doesn't even think of them as anything other than normal. The disorder can be quite incapacitating and difficult to treat. It is possible to suffer from major depression and dysthymia at the same time—the so-called double depression. Some teenagers move from a dysthymic state to a major depression and back again without ever feeling healthy. Dysthymia is common in teenagers whose parents suffer from major depression.

Sleep disturbance, appetite and weight changes, and psychomotor symptoms are less common in dysthymia than in major depression. About 10 percent of youngsters with dysthymia will go on to develop major depression within a year. Teenagers suffering from dysthymia may seem cranky and irritable as much as depressed, and have low self-esteem and poor social skills.

Dysthymia (and other kinds of depression as well) interferes with pleasure, and taking pleasure in activities and friends is essential to a teenager's growth and development. Experiencing pleasure—and I am talking about real pleasure, not the superficial satisfaction of desires—allows a youngster to decide what suits her: what sports, what activities, what books, what kind of schoolwork, what kinds of friends are important or valuable. Pleasure tells a teenager when things are working right. If he has an illness that is preventing him from experiencing pleasure, this can be a serious detriment to normal development. In a sense, he's missing the feedback that tells him what's good for him. This is happening precisely at a time of life when the youngster must establish a separate sense of self in preparation for adulthood.

Premenstrual Dysphoric Disorder

The symptoms of this form of depression occur regularly in the week before the beginning of the menstrual flow in most cycles, and begin to remit within a few days of the onset of menstruation. These symptoms are much more severe than those of premenstrual syndrome (PMS) and interfere with functioning with the family, at school, or at work. The young woman feels sad or hopeless, tense or anxious. She may be persistently irritable or angry, and her mood may change frequently. She may also feel fatigued, socially withdrawn, overwhelmed, unable to concentrate, or out of control. The symptoms can be accompanied by thoughts of suicide. In other words, the symptoms can be of comparable severity to those of major depression, although they do not last as long.

There is some evidence that girls with premenstrual dysphoric disorder (PMDD) are at increased risk for later developing major depression in connection with postpartum periods and the years immediately preceding menopause. In one study, college freshmen with premenstrual symptoms—depression or irritability, not physical symptoms like menstrual cramps—were twice as likely as those without such symptoms to have had a serious depressive episode in the past, and 7 percent of the teenagers with these premenstrual symptoms, and none of the controls, had an affective episode during the ensuing year.

The issue of depression and hormonal change is complex. Hormonal changes, whether caused by the arrival of menarche, by going on (or off) birth control pills, or by other causes, are associated with depression, even though they are not, strictly speaking, a cause of the illness. The psychiatrist diagnosing PMDD or another mood disorder in a teenage girl must carefully distinguish it from the normal transient mood changes that many young women experience around the time they get their period or at the start of menarche. Although the DSM-IV does not now classify PMDD as a disease (it is called a "disorder requiring further study") many mental health professionals treat it successfully using a combination of diet, exercise, and antidepressant medicine.

Bipolar Disorder

Sometimes called manic-depressive illness, this is a complex disorder, difficult to diagnose in teenagers, and extremely variable in its symptoms. The standard text on the disease, *Manic Depressive Illness* (one of whose authors, Kay Redfield Jamison, herself suffers from bipolar disorder and has published a memoir, *An Unquiet Mind*, about it), is more than nine hundred pages of double-column text, charts, diagrams, and references. Although ascertaining exact numbers of people who suffer from it is difficult, the disease is not as rare as might be expected. Yet fewer than one in three of those suffering from it will ever be properly treated for it. The younger the age at which depression first appears, the more likely bipolar illness is to develop.

Very generally speaking, bipolar disorder is characterized by cycling moods of depression and mania—irrational elation, frenzied activity, excitability, or anger—over a period of at least a year. In the depressive phase, the symptoms are indistinguishable from major depression. Reduced appetite and insomnia are common during the manic phase, increased appetite and increased need for sleep during the depressive phase. The manic phase is characterized by abnormal expansiveness of mood, excessive energy, poor judgment in social or school situations, and an optimism and self-confidence inappropriate to the circumstances. The youngster afflicted may engage in activities that have a high potential for disastrous outcome—reckless driving, for example, or alcohol and drug abuse.

She may do her schoolwork enthusiastically and quickly, but in a disorganized way. Teenagers who are manic may start numerous projects with great enthusiasm but carry none of them to a conclusion, act fresh and talk too fast and too loudly, become overconfident of their abilities, have difficulty sleeping but nevertheless not feel tired. Promiscuity can also be a problem, especially for girls in a manic state. This kind of behavior in young women also becomes a defense against the depression that they fear is to come.

This is a recurrent disorder—more than 90 percent of people who have had a single manic episode go on to have another, an average of four in ten years. The cycles vary in length: in the "rapid cycling" form of the disease, four or more mood episodes occur in a year. To complicate matters further, the mood changes may not actually alternate. Since even healthy teenagers have rapidly changing moods, the disease may be difficult to diagnose in this age group, and bipolar disorder can be confused with conduct disorder, attention deficit hyperactivity disorder, or, when hallucinations or other psychotic symptoms are present, schizophrenia. Most studies find that 20 to 30 percent of adults with bipolar illness had similar symptoms as teenagers. About 10 percent to 15 percent of teenagers who have recurrent episodes of major depression will go on to develop bipolar illness.

The symptoms of the illness vary greatly. Some patients' moods cycle more frequently than others; some switch rapidly from one mood to another without an intervening period of normal mood. There can also be "mixed" episodes—moods that have both depressive and manic characteristics. The length of an episode and the time between episodes are both highly variable. Sometimes a patient can be symptom-free for years after the first episode; the first episode itself may be depressive or manic, or a combination of the two. In females, the first episode is more likely to be depressive; in males it is more likely to be manic.

The periods of irrational elation in this illness are called either "manic" or "hypomanic" episodes, with hypomanic episodes being of shorter duration and milder symptoms than manic episodes. The

DSM-IV divides bipolar illness into two separate illnesses: Bipolar I and Bipolar II. Bipolar I has a clinical course that includes manic episodes along with depressive and mixed episodes; Bipolar II disorder includes hypomanic episodes along with one or more depressive episodes. The main difference is the severity of the mania, with the mania in Bipolar II disorder being less severe—hypomanic, as opposed to manic. Bipolar II can look a lot like cyclothymia (see below)—the difference is that in Bipolar II disorder, the youngster has had a full-blown episode of depression.

All of these symptoms can vary greatly from one person to another, and even within the same person from one day to another, and the diagnoses sometimes seem to overlap. I've seen teenagers respond to treatment with everything from barely noticeable change to complete remission of symptoms.

I never jump to conclusions about a bipolar diagnosis because it can only be diagnosed in a teenager after careful observation over a considerable period of time. Often patients who appear depressed do not report prior episodes of mania, and the psychiatrist has to ask about this. Consultation with the family can be an important way to get at the history of the disease and arrive at the right diagnosis. And an accurate diagnosis is essential: the treatment for manic-depressive illness is different from that for depression, and if the disorder is mistaken for depression and only the depressive symptoms are treated, a full-blown manic episode may result. Unlike major depression, which is more common in girls, bipolar illness is equally common in boys and girls.

Bipolar disorder and cyclothymia are much harder to diagnose in a teenager than they are in an adult. Adolescents are often moody for developmental reasons that have nothing to do with disease. A swiftly changing mood from morose to elated in an adult means one thing; in a teenager, it can mean something else entirely. It is only when a youngster's changing moods are severe, when they persist over long periods of time, and when they interfere with normal school or social activities that I begin to suspect that psychiatric treatment may be the answer. Teenagers' emotions can be difficult to live with—any adolescent can be, as almost any parent will attest, "impossible." But being "impossible" is not a psychiatric symptom or a psychiatric diagnosis—it is an expected part of adolescent development. Distinguishing this kind of normal development from true psychiatric illness is a constant challenge with adolescents, and doing so successfully requires both training and clinical experience.

Although there are effective drug treatments for manic-depressive illness—lithium and other mood stabilizers in carefully regulated doses—their action remains somewhat mysterious, and compliance with treatment is far from a foregone conclusion. The drugs alleviate both of the disease's radically different symptoms—the depression and the irrational elation—but for an adolescent, getting rid of the depressive state may not compensate for the simultaneous banishment of the manic "highs" the disorder produces, which, especially during their milder stages, can be quite pleasurable and even constructive. There is evidence that a propensity for bipolar illness is associated with an added degree of creativity, manifested especially in the hypomanic states of the disease.

Bipolar illness, like depression, can be lethal: more than 25 percent of untreated manic-depressive people attempt suicide.

Cyclothymia

Cyclothymia is a milder form of bipolar disorder in which the person cycles through alternating periods of despair and joy, enthusiasm and discouragement, sleepiness and wakefulness, self-confidence and self-pity, laughing and crying. The disease goes on for at least a year in adolescents, and symptom-free periods last no longer than eight weeks.

Teenagers suffering from this disorder might show predominately hypomanic symptoms, predominately depressed symptoms, or mixed symptoms, and the timing of the cycles can vary considerably. Often a parent, seeing the first clinical symptoms of cyclothymia, will tell me their youngster is "high-strung" or "hyperactive" or "very moody." The periods of hypomanic symptoms—the "high" periods—

in this disorder do not meet the criteria for a manic episode, and the "lows" are not as severe or long-lasting as those of major depression. If a teenager later has a full-blown episode of mania or major depression, her diagnosis will be changed to bipolar disorder.

Teenagers can be intense, impulsive, grandiose, provocative, self-absorbed, secretive, guarded, withdrawn. They can be risk-takers and thrill-seekers, often because they have the physical capacities of adults without adult problem-solving skills or judgment. They can be hypersensitive and callous at the same time. They can be excessively self-conscious, easily humiliated, overly concerned with their physical appearance, contemptuous even of those closest to them and especially so of their parents. In an adult, characteristics like these might suggest what psychiatrists call a "character disorder" or a "personality disorder," traits of personality so dysfunctional or socially unacceptable that they actually lead to a psychiatric diagnosis. But in kids, all of these things can be merely a part of ordinary development. In a sense, a teenager hasn't had a long enough history to reveal to a therapist what is personality and what is a temporary mood or developmental stage, and the younger a teenager is the harder it is to tell. Few therapists would diagnose a personality disorder in a teenager who exhibited such characteristics, and unless these characteristics interfered with normal functioning or were accompanied by behavior like truancy, running away from home, petty crime, or drug or alcohol abuse, most psychiatrists wouldn't diagnose any psychiatric illness at all. In thinking about the other forms of depression (see below), these considerations are foremost in the psychiatrist's mind.

IN THEIR OWN WORDS:
A PERMANENT STATE OF ANTICLIMAX

Being depressed is like living in a permanent state of anticlimax. It's not some great, crashing thing that makes you violently angry in a thrashing madman sort of way. It's more of a slow-moving son-ofabitch that hits you from behind and works its merry way around you.

—Julia, age 14

Other Forms of Depression

Since even the mildest forms of depression can cause significant problems, they are also being studied. These illnesses—recurrent brief depressive disorder and minor depressive disorder—are listed in the appendix to the DSM-IV. Although milder or briefer than the disorders already discussed, they can be serious illnesses. Both these disorders can begin in adolescence and are associated with increased risk for suicide. Usually, one or two of the symptoms of depression are present in these forms, but not enough to meet the criteria for major depression.

DIAGNOSING DEPRESSION

So how do I know if a teenager has clinical depression? Any doctor will make his own observations of the patient, and so will a psychiatrist, but as in almost any other field of medicine, one of the first questions, phrased in one way or another, is "Where does it hurt?" Although my patient will be unlikely to point to a specific part of her body, reports of what she is feeling are essential. To be called "major depression" the depressive episode has to last for at least two weeks, during which the teenager feels in an extremely low mood or has a complete loss of interest in activities and pursuits that once gave her pleasure. In teenagers, as distinct from adults, this low mood can be characterized by irritability rather than sadness. I elicit this information from the teenager, and I take into account reports by the parents. But an irritable mood that persists for two weeks, however unpleasant, is not by itself a reason to conclude that the youngster suffers from depression—there can be lots of reasons in a teenager's life for a persistent bad mood. So to conclude that depression is the problem, other symptoms must also be present.

To be characterized as an episode of major depression, the depressed mood must persist for most of the day, nearly every day, an observation made by others or by the patient him- or herself. The depressed teenager feels a radically diminished pleasure in almost all activities, and feels this way every day. Appetite changes are another symptom—gaining or losing significant amounts of weight in a short period (5 percent of body weight in one month) is yet another suggestion that depression may be the cause. Sleeping too much—hypersomnia, as it is called—or insomnia are also symptoms of depression. Being agitated or slowed down is another symptom, but this must be more than just a subjective feeling—others must be able to observe this change in the youngster. Extreme fatigue or loss of energy nearly every day is another sign. Excessive guilt inappropriate to the circumstances can be a symptom, but the guilt must be felt almost every day, and must be more than just ordinary self-reproach or guilt about feeling sick and thus being a burden to others. If the teenager herself or others notice an extreme inability to concentrate, this can be a symptom, too, but of course must be distinguished from ordinary restlessness that teenagers (and others, for that matter) may occasionally feel. Finally, recurrent thoughts about death, recurrent thoughts of suicide, making plans to commit suicide, or actual suicide attempts are not only symptoms but emergencies that require immediate professional medical attention.

When a psychiatrist detects five or more of these symptoms, he or she arrives at a diagnosis: the problem is that the teenager is suffering from major depression. Of course, I don't hold a list in my hands, and check it off as I examine the patient. Nor do I simply ask the youngster how he feels in the vague way I might if I were a friend or an interested adult. The examination of the patient, like any medical examination, is systematic, covering specific points of behavior and physical functioning that the doctor knows point to depression. The experienced psychiatrist carries on a conversation that will elicit these reports from the patient. Psychiatrists who lack experience, or are just starting out, may feel they have to ask each question as if they were filling out a form. This, as you might imagine, works badly with kids who are already emotionally distressed. It requires great skill on the part of the doctor to elicit from a teenager the responses that will suggest a diagnosis.

Depression Scales

A therapist's clinical judgment, backed by knowledge of differential diagnosis, is the primary way of figuring out if a teenager is suffering from depression. But rating scales can give a degree of objectivity to estimating the progress of treatment. There are scales that can be used by the therapist, and some that can be used by the teenager to provide a tangible record of feelings and symptoms.

Among the most widely used clinician-rated scales are the Hamilton Depression Scale and the Montgomery and Osberg Depression Rating Scale. The Hamilton Scale measures mood, feelings of guilt, suicidal ideas, sleep disorders, changes in schoolwork, and so on, with the clinician assigning a number from 0 to 4 to estimate the intensity of each of these cognitive or behavioral symptoms. The Montgomery and Osberg is useful for measuring the success of antidepressant treatment. It includes ratings of pessimistic thoughts, self-accusation, remorse, guilt, self-reproach, and other indicators of depression which are rated on a 7-point scale.

A teenager can also rate herself using standardized scales. Among tests designed for this purpose are the Beck Depression Inventory, the Zung Self-Rating Depression Scale, the Carroll Rating Scale, and the Inventory for Depressive Symptomatology. Typically, these scales list statements ("I feel the world would be better off without me," "I have thoughts of harming myself, but I would not carry them out," "I have trouble sleeping through the night," and so on) and the teenager rates herself on whether the statements apply to her.

Psychologists, rather than psychiatrists, are usually the professionals who administer these tests, and using and interpreting them requires extensive training and considerable sophistication—they are not parlor games or quizzes designed for a popular magazine.

Mild depression involves symptoms that just barely meet the criteria and cause only minor functional impairment. These are of course the most difficult to detect in teenagers, who may be mildly moody in any case. In more severe cases, symptoms begin to interfere with daily life, and the most severe cases of major depression result in actual disability—the inability to go to school, maintain friendships, or pursue the ordinary tasks of everyday teenage life.

It may not be obvious that any of these things is happening to a teenager. A youngster can easily conceal feelings from a parent, from a therapist, and even from himself. Often a youngster I'm talking to will deny feeling down in the dumps, until I point out that he looks as if he's on the verge of crying. Not everyone describes a bad mood in the same way, either. Some kids say they feel nothing, just "kind of blah." Others will stress some physical complaint rather than a feeling of sadness. Depressed teenagers often feel angry rather than sad—everything sets them off with an angry outburst or an accusation; even the smallest setback results in frustrated rage.

Diagnosing depression or any other psychiatric illness correctly is difficult and complicated. To do it successfully requires years of reading, training, and clinical experience, and even experienced mental health professionals make mistakes. As with any serious disease, choosing the right therapist is essential.

3

Which Teenagers Are Most at Risk?

No one can yet identify a single cause for depression, but studies have shown that there are certain risk factors that increase the likelihood of a teenager becoming clinically depressed. Having a risk factor doesn't mean that you'll get the disease, only that statistically your chances of getting it increase. The concept of risk factors, which applies to many diseases, both medical and psychiatric, is sometimes difficult to understand. If you smoke cigarettes, for example, you radically increase your risk of getting lung cancer, a risk that is tiny if you don't smoke—even though most people who smoke cigarettes don't get lung cancer. Only a minority of people with the risk factors for depression will actually get the illness, but the more risk factors a youngster has, the greater the chance of her becoming ill.

GENES AND DEPRESSION

You may be concerned that because you or someone else in your family has suffered from depression, that your child will too. There is almost certainly a genetic component to the disease passed on by parents to children, and this genetic component, under the right circumstances, contributes to the development of clinical depression in a youngster. But this does not mean that the cause of the teenager's depression is his parents. Rather, having parents who are depressed is a risk factor among many others suggesting that one adolescent may be more susceptible than another.

A 1997 study showed that families of depressed youths were five times as likely as those of non-depressed kids to have someone in the family who also suffers from depression. The closer the relative who was depressed, the more likely the child was to be depressed, and a female relative's depression was a better predictor of depression in the youngster than that of a male relative. Other studies have found that the presence of depression in parents predicts not only psychiatric but also medical illnesses in children, including headaches, respiratory disorders, and genitourinary disorders.

Having two parents who are depressed substantially increases the risk of depression in their offspring—according to one study, the likelihood changes from about 30 percent with one parent to about 70 percent with two.

The conclusion that depression is at least partly a genetic illness derives from statistical studies, not laboratory findings. Although no one has actually located a "depression gene" that is inherited from one generation to another, the search for physical evidence of the genetic connection continues. Few researchers expect to find a single gene responsible for the illness, and most acknowledge that even finding a gene that, for example, alters the production of neurotransmitters in some way, will not "explain" depression. Depression, like many diseases, is undoubtedly the result of a complex interaction of genes and environment.

There is some evidence to suggest that depression is inherited on the X chromosome, which would help explain why women suffer from depression more commonly than men (women have two X chromosomes, men one X and one Y). But there is also evidence that depression can be inherited through the male line, from father to son, so this cannot be the only explanation. One group of researchers, working with the Old Order Amish of Pennsylvania, a genetically homogeneous population, did find a specific genetic marker associated with depression, but it is not the single "depression gene." Twin studies offer further proof: if one identical twin is depressed, the other is highly likely to be depressed as well, and this appears to be true even with identical twins who are raised apart in different environments.

At least one study followed adolescents over a ten-year period to try to determine more precisely how much risk is increased by having a parent who is depressed. The researchers found a three times greater risk for major depressive disorder and phobias. Sadly, the study also showed that the depressed offspring of depressed parents were less likely to seek treatment than the depressed offspring of non-depressed parents.

In short, the details are still much in question, but the general principle is widely agreed upon: clinical depression can be inherited. It is therefore important for parents to know that a family history of depression is a warning and that early intervention with teenagers can spare them much unnecessary suffering.

STRESSFUL EVENTS

If a teenager fails a test in school, ends a romantic relationship, or suffers the death of a loved one or the divorce of his parents, these things can get him depressed—but that doesn't mean he has major depression. Even though some teenagers imagine for a time that not getting into their first-choice college or failing a math test means the end of the world, and may even dramatically express such thoughts, they soon realize that that isn't so. They figure out a way to make up for the failure, choose another college, begin a new relationship, reconcile themselves to the loss—they get over the setback, and go back to normal life. But for some adolescents this sort of sad but common event can be the initiating factor in an episode of serious illness that then takes on a life of its own, bearing little or no connection to the event or events that precipitated it.

No one expects a teenager to grin and bear it with every setback—life has sad events that anyone is entitled to feel sad about. But if the sadness or grief is out of proportion to the event, or lasts much longer than seems normal or appropriate, or gives way to physical symptoms, then there may be a more serious problem to be dealt with.

OUT OF PROPORTION

Matt was a well-adjusted, happy kid when two things happened. His parents separated, and his father was diagnosed with early (and treatable) colon cancer. Within a couple of months of these two events, Matt was hospitalized with depression. His entire life had become unsafe, his near-perfect world was falling apart: his parents were splitting up, and one of them was, at least in Matt's view, fatally ill. Although Matt had never had a depression before, these two events provoked an episode. Every kid reacts to problems like these in his own way; some, like Matt, become seriously ill.

What is a stressor and what is not? This is a question that a teenager will answer very differently from an adult. A bad grade in a math course may seem a rather minor matter from a vantage point thirty years after the event, but at the moment it happens to an adolescent, it can, for some kids, be extremely stressful. Divorce, remarriage, new or combined families—these are of course common events in American life today that most kids can handle (if not always easily or gracefully), but in some vulnerable kids, disruptions like these can provoke an episode of depression.

Bereavement

There have been several large studies of bereaved children and adolescents, and most suggest that in the months immediately after the death of a parent a significant percentage of these kids meet the symptomatic criteria for major depression. Interestingly, when the kids were interviewed directly, they reported significantly more depressive symptoms than their surviving parents had noticed. All of these studies included a wide age range, from small children through late adolescence.

But bereavement is not depression, however sad it may be. Unless the bereavement is unusually extended in length or leads to persistent behavioral problems, a therapist would not treat this as an episode of depression. What an adolescent in such circumstances needs is the sympathy and understanding of family and friends. Bereavement counseling can also prove useful.

ANXIETY

About 20 percent of adolescents who suffer from depression also suffer from anxiety disorder. These young people suffer not just from normal worries—nervousness about making friends, fears of failure on an exam, and so on—but from an overwhelming and paralyzing fear that grips them for as long as six months at a time, an anxiety far out of proportion to any of the things they feel anxious about. Worry dominates their lives and interferes with normal activities: they can think of little else except their worries. The worrying affects their concentration and is often directed not at especially nervous-making events but at the routine tasks of daily life: getting to class on time, finishing a homework assignment, and so on. Often, they worry about their own competence; they are sure they are going to fail, no matter how hard they work or how carefully they prepare. Sometimes they worry excessively and irrationally about harm that may come to them or other family members by being away from home.

Physical symptoms are also common: there may be trembling, feeling shaky, muscle aches, or soreness. Dry mouth, sweating, clammy hands, a "lump in the throat," nausea, and diarrhea often accompany anxiety disorder.

Depression is a separate issue, but it often accompanies or follows this kind of severe anxiety, and the symptoms of the two illnesses can overlap. If a youngster experiences this kind of anxiety, he is also at risk for depression. See chapter 5 for a further discussion of the connection between anxiety and depression.

ANXIETY AND DEPRESSION AT THE SAME TIME

Jodi was a sophomore in college who one day in the middle of an English class, for no apparent reason, had a panic attack, a form of severe anxiety characterized by extreme fear and overwhelming physical symptoms such as shortness of breath and palpitations. She left the class terrified, and went to the infirmary where a nurse managed to calm her down. She went back to her room and called her parents to tell them what happened. By this time she had pretty much recovered, and the next day went to class without incident. But when she got into her car to go home, she had another panic attack, even more severe than the first one. She pulled over to the side of the road, and her parents had to come and get her.

Her parents took her to the family doctor, who, after a series of tests, reassured her that she had nothing physically wrong with her. Unfortunately, this only confirmed her fears that she was going crazy.

The disorder became more and more disabling. She became afraid to do anything—she couldn't even leave her house without being terrified. Then, she developed full-blown depressive symptoms. At this point, her parents called me for an appointment. When I first saw her, the most immediate goal was to get her incapacitating anxiety symptoms under control. I started her on the benzodiazapine Ativan for the acute episodes of panic, as well as the SSRI antidepressant Zoloft, which works for both depression and panic disorder (see chapter 8 for a full discussion of medicines for depression). Although we started with a low dose of Zoloft, I eventually increased it to almost the maximum. The Ativan was gradually tapered because, although it is effective for anxiety, it is addictive and must be used with caution because of its potential for abuse. Ativan can be used when necessary to prevent the development of a full-blown panic attack when the patient begins to feel one coming on, and Jodi carried a single pill with her for such emergencies.

I see this often in young women, and both the anxiety and the depression must be treated. If you only treat the depression, the disabling anxiety may remain even after the depression lifts. While the newer SSRIs are useful for anxiety, you sometimes need more. In Jodi's case, Ativan proved useful in combination with Zoloft.

CONDUCT DISORDER

The DSM-IV's description of this disorder paints a picture of a truly "bad" kid—the kind of teenager feared as much by his peers as by his parents and other adults. He threatens other kids, bullies them when he can, initiates physical fights with little or no provocation. He is physically cruel to people and animals, steals from people while confronting them (for example, mugging or extortion). He may have forced someone into sexual activity. He destroys property with the intention of causing serious and expensive damage, engages in deceitful behavior, lies to obtain goods or favors. He may break into houses or cars, stay out at night despite parental prohibitions, set fires. School truancy is a habit, and these kids may run away from home more than once. These teenagers are dangerous both to themselves and others, since kids who are violent toward others have extremely high rates of suicide.

For better or worse, youngsters like these are as often dealt with by police and judges as by the mental health system, and the debate over whether these children are "psychologically disturbed" and in need of treatment or "just plain criminals" and in need of incarceration will not be resolved here. But in any case, it is demonstrably true that depression is common among youngsters like these, whether we think they're suffering from any other diagnosable psychiatric illness or not. In samples of depressed teenagers, about 10 percent are found to have conduct disorder as well.

A parent with a teenager like this will welcome any help possible that obviates the need for putting the child in jail or some form of juvenile detention. Depression doesn't cause kids to have a conduct disorder—most kids who are depressed never engage in behavior even remotely resembling this—but depression often enough accompanies conduct disorder. Bipolar disorder, especially in its manic and hypomanic periods, can lead to conduct problems as well, and conduct disorder may be confused with or made worse by untreated bipolar disorder. These are certainly things to look for in kids who are seriously acting up, and treating depression (or bipolar disorder) is essential even if it doesn't solve all problems.

SEXUAL ABUSE

Childhood sexual abuse is associated with depression in children, teenagers, and adults. In preschool children, this may be the most common cause of serious depression. One study found that risk for suicide was eight times greater for teenagers with a history of sexual abuse than for those without, and that adolescence was the most vulnerable period for suicide attempts. Sexual abuse is also the most common stressor in post-traumatic stress disorder (PTSD) in teenagers, and girls are more likely to develop PTSD than boys. Adolescents who are hospitalized have higher rates of childhood neglect and abuse.

Although an adolescent may not be able to report directly a history of sexual abuse, in the course of a thorough interview with a suicidal adolescent, such details may emerge.

SEXUAL ABUSE AND SUICIDE

Alison was the oldest of four children, born into a solidly middle-class intact family in which her father worked and her mother was a homemaker. I first met her following a serious suicide attempt, after she was hospitalized for overdosing on a large number of pills prescribed by her outpatient psychiatrist. At age 16 she had been in treatment for alcoholism and depression for about two years. Only in the past month had she revealed to her therapist a history of repeated sexual abuse by a family friend from age 5 to 10. Once she began talking about this she developed intense feelings of guilt, shame, and self-loathing. Believing that revealing the secret to her parents would cause her family unbearable agony, she decided the only solution was suicide. She hoarded her antidepressants and anti-anxiety medications until she felt that she had a lethal dose. Then she wrote a note to her parents asking them to forgive her, and swallowed the pills. A younger sibling came home from school early, and found her unresponsive. She was brought to the hospital and treated in the intensive care unit. Since that time, she has had two more near-fatal suicide attempts despite intensive psychiatric treatment. She has also developed symptoms of post-traumatic stress disorder, including nightmares, flashbacks, and emotional numbing.

THOUGHTS OF DEATH AND SUICIDE

Chapter 4 contains an extensive discussion of suicide, so we won't go into detail here. Suffice it to say for the moment that most teenagers who attempt suicide are suffering from depression, and that any attempt at suicide, or even a suicide threat, is a medical emergency that demands immediate attention. Ruling out depression as a cause of this behavior will be a high priority, and if depression is the cause, then treating it quickly and effectively is crucial.

Even without an actual suicide attempt, almost half of depressed teenagers have thoughts of death or express a wish to be dead. These thoughts and wishes, no matter to whom they are expressed, must be taken seriously as possible indicators of suicide risk. Sometimes a teenager will keep these thoughts to herself, and a parent will have to elicit the feelings with a direct question. If you suspect a teenager is harboring such thoughts, ask her. This is not something a youngster should be allowed to keep to herself.

Talking to a Depressed Teenager

Depressed people are not fun to be around—it's easier to stay away from them until they feel better. But making it clear that you are determined to listen to her problems can make life a lot easier for a depressed teenager. This requires tremendous patience, thoughtful listening, and responses that make sense. Telling a depressed youngster to "cheer up and get on with it" won't help: this kind of advice just isn't useful to people suffering from depression. Better to sympathize, recognize that she is expressing genuine feelings, offer reassuring words, remind her that things will get better, that the way she feels now is not the way she will always feel, even if she finds that hard to believe. Save argument, criticism, and blame for another time. This is a time for encouragement and praise, understanding and commiseration. Sometimes parents attempt to "reason" adolescents out of their feelings, telling them that "it doesn't make any sense to feel that way." This is not helpful, either, and may only serve to make the youngster stop talking to you. Kids are entitled to their feelings, no matter how irrational, and parents must recognize this.

It is especially important to know if the teenager has thought of harming himself. Parents may be completely unaware that their teenager has thought of committing suicide—many kids, even kids who are highly verbal and expressive, just keep it to themselves. Asking directly is the best way to find out.

IMPAIRMENTS IN SOCIAL FUNCTIONING

Kids operate in three areas that are quite separate: at home, with friends, and at school. While a teenager's behavior at home is obvious to his parents, they don't always know what's happening elsewhere. Friends may be unaware of problems at home, the school authorities may be unaware of problems with peers, and parents may be ignorant of both their youngster's relationship with friends and the extent of academic difficulties. Even when they make a conscientious effort to find out how their teenager is doing, parents are not always the most objective observers, quite naturally preferring to see most things in the best possible light.

My patient Joe provides an example. He was 17 when his mother died in a car accident, but he was the kind of kid who could handle adversity. Despite the shock, he had done reasonably well after the death; he got busy taking care of his younger brother, kept up relationships with his large circle of friends, and functioned well academically and athletically, as he always had. His father couldn't handle living in the same house after his wife died, so they moved, and Joe had to change schools—a change that can cause problems for adolescents, but Joe seemed to take it in stride. About a year after his mother's death, his father married the widow of a close friend who had died several years ago.

Although no one seemed to notice, Joe suddenly became increasingly driven to do well at sports, spending long hours working out or running at the track. He also began an independent study project that kept him up late writing and doing research on the Internet. Right after he was accepted by Stanford (and was trying to decide whether a state school would be better because of the expense), he drank half a bottle of vodka and got in his car with the intention of driving it into the nearest telephone pole. Fortunately, his father noticed him attempting to weave out of the driveway, and stopped him before he could leave.

Joe had always been a good kid, and even when things started to go bad for him he successfully concealed his feelings. No one knew how much the death of his mother and the subsequent losses and disruptions in his life had begun to trouble him until it was almost too late. He took everyone, even those closest to him, by surprise. Fortunately, his suicide plan was aborted, and he was psychiatrically hospitalized and successfully treated for depression.

With other kids the problems seem obvious, even if it isn't obvious at first that depression is the problem. Betsy is 15. She came to treatment because her parents were concerned about her emotional outbursts at home. She was getting into verbal and even physical fights with her siblings. She was completely defiant, wouldn't obey phone rules or curfews, once tore the phone off the wall when her father asked her to conclude a phone call, punched her sister several times, and generally acted impossible when she wasn't actually violent. She had become obsessed with her boyfriend (often the reason for unreasonably long phone conversations). Her parents understood that rebellion is a normal part of growing up—that kids have to separate themselves from adults in order to achieve independence. But they also knew that this kind of violent rebellion was not normal. They needed help with her, and they needed it urgently.

At first, she was unwilling to come into treatment—the problem was not her, but her parents, her siblings, her boyfriend. The family felt otherwise and were on the verge of having her hospitalized because her behavior had become so irrational. She was given an ultimatum: either you go for an evaluation or the police will be called the next time you're out of control. She agreed to come in. Outside of the house, she seemed a little isolated, but otherwise she looked fine. At home, she was out of control.

One of the first things I learned about Betsy was that she hadn't been sleeping well for months—obsessive racing thoughts were keeping her awake every night. She hadn't been able to concentrate well at school, either, and work that had been easy before was now becoming more and more difficult. The only time she felt "normal" was when she was with her boyfriend. Otherwise, she felt discouraged and angry. She was pretty much a model citizen, no alcohol or drug use, no smoking, not even having sex with her boyfriend. But she was in serious trouble anyway: in the course of the evaluation, it became clear that she was depressed. She lived with her father and stepmother and had been dealing with issues of abandonment—her biological mother had been an alcoholic who had left her and her sisters. She thought that her father sided with her sisters and step-mother and that he didn't care about what she was doing or feeling. She was holding on to the boyfriend as the only constant object in her life—and he was pulling away because of her neediness.

Once given the opportunity to speak, she was eager to pursue treatment. When she realized that there were pieces of the puzzle that could be put together, she attended sessions conscientiously, took her medicine, and worked hard in psychotherapy. She is still in treatment; she still takes her medication.

Betsy was unable to control her impulses. She wasn't sleeping. She was obsessing about her boyfriend. All of these were symptoms of depression, and she improved dramatically with antidepressant medication and psychotherapy.

Whether or not parents are the first to notice it, most kids who are depressed will function poorly in at least one of these three domains—at home, at school, or with friends—and many will function poorly in all of them. A recent study showed that these kinds of impairments are among the most common symptoms in depressed teenagers, much more common than anxiety disorders, disruptive behavior disorders, or dysthymia.

The probability of combined disorders—"comorbid," as doctors call them—increases with the severity of depression. Dysthymia, anxiety disorders, suicide attempts, and failures in social functioning are common in depressed youngsters, and the probability of one or more of these increases with the severity of the depression. Yet only a minority of teenagers are treated for the depression that may be the most significant and treatable problem they face.

I've described in this chapter some of the factors—both genetic and behavioral—that may lead you to suspect a youngster is suffering from depression. In the next chapter, I'll discuss in some detail the single most terrifying possible outcome of a depression left untreated: suicide.

4

Suicide

If you ask people to name the most common reason why people under 35 are admitted to hospitals, few will get the right answer: suicide attempts. Between 1950 and 1983, the suicide rate among teenagers quadrupled, and although it has begun to fall slightly in recent years, it remains a major problem: 20 percent of male suicides and 14 percent of female suicides occur in the age group of 15 to 24. For adolescents, suicide is the third leading cause of death—just behind car accidents and homicide.

It was once true that suicide rates among white male teenagers were much higher than among black teens. In recent years, however, the rates of suicide among black male adolescents have increased dramatically, and some cities have actually recorded more black male teenage suicides than white. The reasons for this remain obscure. Rates for black female adolescents have, through these years, remained constant and low.

In the 15 to 19 age group (in which 86 percent of teen suicides occur), boys actually kill themselves five times more often than girls, but girls attempt suicide twice as often as boys, most commonly injuring themselves with drug overdoses. Drug overdoses rarely result in completed suicide.

Even with these frightening numbers, the popular press has

exaggerated the contribution of teen suicide to the total number of suicides in the United States. In fact, teenagers, who account for about 14 percent of the population, account for 16 percent of all suicides. In other words, teenagers are only a little more likely to kill themselves than any other age group. Suicide rates are much higher in old age: 20 percent of the population is over 60, and that age group accounts for 40 percent of suicides.

These statistics have to be taken with some skepticism. The actual number of teenagers (and others) who commit suicide is probably much greater than the "official" statistics indicate. Many accidents may actually be covert suicides—illicit drug overdoses that involve teenagers may look more like accidents than they really are; even a fatal car crash can be a suicide. Teenagers also take risks that skirt the edges of suicidal behavior: engaging in dangerous physical activities without adequate preparation or safeguards, testing the limits of alcohol and drug use, performing daredevil athletic feats or dangerous maneuvers in cars or on motorcycles. Death can result from such activities—sometimes intentional and sometimes just as a result of playing Russian roulette without concern about death. There may be emotional, financial, or religious reasons for concealing a suicide, or for wanting to believe it didn't really happen. When there is a violent death, the police are concerned to rule out homicide—once that is done, whether a death is a suicide or not is of less interest from a legal perspective. For all these reasons, there are undoubtedly more suicides than these numbers suggest.

Suicide is of course a subject of much theoretical speculation. Legal experts, physicians, moral philosophers, theologians, novelists, artists, and others throughout history have debated the issue. Can suicide be a rational decision? Does a person have a right to commit suicide? Should a person who wants to commit suicide be prevented from doing so? Is there a state of human misery so irredeemable that suicide is the only reasonable relief? While these questions may be of interest under certain circumstances, they are of no interest at all to the parent of a teenager who wants to harm himself. A parent can only want to stop it from happening.

GUNS AS A HEALTH ISSUE

Here are some facts, elucidated in an important study published in the *Journal of the American Medical Association:*

American adolescents of both sexes are most likely to commit suicide with a firearm—more than two-thirds of teen suicides occur by gun—and the presence of a firearm in the house, whether locked up or not, whether loaded or unloaded, whether a handgun or a rifle, is associated with a higher risk for adolescent suicide, even after controlling for psychiatric variables.

This book takes no position on gun control, but purely as a matter of health, this much is true: choosing to keep a gun in a house where an adolescent lives is a choice for which the health consequences can be disastrous.

STRESS AND SUICIDE

Studies have shown that "acute stressors"—events like school failure, unhappy romantic relationships, physical illness, death of a loved one, and other such things—are considerably overestimated as a cause for adolescent suicide. So when someone says, "Well, no wonder she wanted to commit suicide, look at all the terrible things that were happening to her . . ." this may be "explaining away" rather than truly explaining.

THE PERFECT CHILD

Mary Kate was the epitome of the good child. She excelled in academics and sports, and was extremely popular among her classmates. She was protective of her younger siblings, respectful of adults, was always well behaved and well spoken. When she was 17, she told her parents that she needed to see a psychotherapist.

Her parents were astonished. Why would anyone like her need psychotherapy? At first they resisted, but eventually they came to see me. It was only after several sessions that she was able to reveal what was troubling her.

Over the past several years she had begun to use drugs, initially only intermittently, but then more consistently. She limited her use, however, to weekends when her parents weren't around. The month before she came to see me she had become so distraught that she deliberately got as high as she could, then tried to drive her car. Her friends stopped her just in time.

The reasons for her actions only gradually became clear. She felt pressure from all sides: her parents could accept nothing less than superior academic performance; her field hockey coach expected her to play even when injured; her friends made constant demands on her attention which she felt obliged to fulfill. Finally she decided she couldn't live up to everyone's expectations and summoned the nerve to kill herself. Even this was to be a perfect act: if she died in a car accident, she had determined, no one would ever know that she had done it deliberately.

Many studies have shown that suicide in the absence of serious psychiatric illness is extremely rare among adolescents. This doesn't mean that an unhappy event can't by itself lead to suicide—it undoubtedly can. But an unhappy event, or even multiple unhappy events, in a teenager's life are not in themselves a cause of suicide, and experiencing stressful events is not a predictor of which teenagers are going to kill themselves. I try to avoid such "explanations" when considering a patient who has attempted suicide, even when there is a clear stressor preceding the attempt. When the family or the therapist of a suicide victim or attempter looks back for causes and finds an "acute stressor" of some kind, I want to know whether that stressor was itself a product of a psychiatric illness.

Studies that compare suicide victims to other adolescents afflicted with matching psychiatric disorders find no way to distinguish between living patients and suicide victims by looking at the stressful events that have occurred in their lives. Suicide, or attempted suicide, is in almost all cases the result of a psychiatric disorder, not an unhappy life event.

So stress itself does not cause suicide. Psychiatric illness is more likely the cause of both the poorly handled stress and the suicide that follows it. This distinction has important clinical implications that parents and teenagers (not to mention their doctors) must understand. If a youngster attempts suicide after a stressful life event, it may be a dangerous mistake to attribute the attempt to that specific stress, concluding that since the event is over with, so is the danger of suicide. This dismisses the much more likely possibility that psychiatric illness is the cause and leaves the teenager in a continuing precarious position.

The most common psychiatric disorders found in suicides and suicide attempters are depression and alcohol abuse. Studies show varying results, but roughly one-third to one-half of teen suicide victims have major depression; alcohol or other substance abuse plays a role in more than half of all suicides among teenagers.

SUICIDE CLUSTERS AND "COPYCAT" SUICIDES

It always seems, from reading the papers, that when there is one well-publicized teenage suicide, more follow, a kind of suicide contagion that seems to be more severe the more extensive the press coverage of the original death. In the mid-1980s, epidemiologists began to study the idea scientifically. The results of these studies are unanimous: when a suicide is widely discussed in the media, there is a predictable increase in adolescent suicide within the ensuing two weeks. At least a half-dozen different studies show that prominent display of a suicide in the media leads to an increase in suicidal deaths, and the more TV stations or newspapers that carry or repeat the story, the more suicides there are. Even fictional depictions of adolescent suicide on TV lead to more suicides and suicide attempts.

What is it about teenagers that makes them imitate suicide in a way that adults never do? Adolescents appear to view suicide as romantic, perhaps the more so when the suicide is that of a famous person they admire—a rock star, for example. The singer Kurt Cobain's suicide provoked this kind of phenomenon among a certain number of his teenage fans. Adolescents fail to understand the effect suicide will have on the people who love them. I can remember being in a room with a teenage suicide attempter, recovered and apparently at ease, as his distraught family members sat with him, stricken, crying, almost in mourning. The adolescent in question clearly had no idea how profoundly his actions would affect his family, and little understanding of their reaction even when he saw it.

Studies have tested many other explanations for suicide clusters—maybe prior conditions were such that a wave of suicides was inevitable; maybe the stories about suicide were only moving people to suicide who would have committed suicide even without them; maybe, after a prominent suicide, the police start classifying deaths as suicides that would otherwise be classified as accidents; maybe it's grief, rather than copycat suicide, that provokes the increase; maybe it's just a statistically random event, like the "cancer clusters" the press reports from time to time. Each explanation in turn has been proven incorrect. The sad fact is that kids do copy a well-publicized suicide, and it happens only among teenagers, not adults. Girls are more likely to commit copycat suicide than boys, and whether the story is about a specific suicide or just a general story about the phenomenon of suicide makes little or no difference.

The suicidal death of a friend or relative, particularly that of a parent, may also increase risk for suicide in vulnerable youngsters. In these circumstances, helping a youngster understand that suicide is an unsatisfactory coping strategy and aiding him in reducing any guilt or social isolation he may feel are useful interventions that not only mental health professionals but school counselors, parents, and friends can be involved in.

No one should conclude that talking to a teenager about his or her own suicidal feelings has the same effect. There's no evidence that it does. There is a vast difference between sitting and watching a televised report of a suicide about which a teenager can fantasize on the one hand, and an interactive dialogue with a parent or a professional about a youngster's own experience on the other. The two should not be confused.

SUICIDE WARNING SIGNS

Although it is almost impossible to predict precisely which teenager will attempt suicide, there are warning signs that parents can look for. The American Academy of Child and Adolescent Psychiatry has assembled this list of indications. If one or more of these signs occurs, parents should talk to their teenager and seek professional help.

- Unusual changes in eating and sleeping habits
- Withdrawal from friends, family, and regular activities
- Violent actions, rebellious behavior, or running away
- Excessive drug and alcohol use
- Unusual neglect of personal appearance
- Marked personality change
- Persistent boredom, difficulty concentrating, or a decline in the quality of schoolwork
- Frequent complaints about physical symptoms, often related to emotions, such as stomachaches, headaches, fatigue, etc.
- Loss of interest in pleasurable activities
- Not tolerating praise or rewards
- Complaints of feeling "rotten inside"

- Giving verbal hints such as "I won't be a problem for you much longer," "Nothing matters," "It's no use," or "I won't be seeing you again."
- Putting his or her affairs in order by giving away favorite possessions, discarding important belongings, cleaning his or her room
- Becoming suddenly cheerful after an episode of depression

ALCOHOL AND DRUGS

In addition to its other well-known dangers for adolescents, alcohol is a high risk factor for suicide. The lifetime risk for suicide is about the same for those suffering from major depression as it is for alcoholics—15 percent—and alcoholics and major depression can, and often do, coexist. There is some evidence that the large increase in adolescent suicide between the mid-1950s and the early 1980s is attributable to increasing rates of alcohol abuse by young people. I certainly see plenty of kids in my practice who are drinking too much and too often. It may be that alcohol use increases the impulsiveness necessary to committing suicide, as it increases impulsiveness in other kinds of behavior, and reduces inhibitions. Some believe that the increases in suicide among male teenagers can be almost completely accounted for by those who committed suicide with discernible levels of alcohol or drugs in their blood.

GENETIC AND BIOLOGICAL FACTORS

There is probably a genetic factor in suicide attempts—people whose parents or close relatives have attempted or completed suicide are more likely than others to do the same, and at least one study has suggested that a trait for suicidal behavior can be transmitted independently of traits for major psychiatric disorders. But of course the issue is extremely complicated. First, it is hard to know whether suicide attempts by kids who have seen suicides in their families are caused by genes, by imitating behaviors, or by both. We know that major depression is in part a genetic illness, so it could be that the genetic connection to suicide is actually a genetic connection to a tendency for major depression or other psychiatric disorders associated with suicide. Or other factors could be involved. Biologic researchers have searched for a clue in neurotransmitters, and disturbances in serotonin metabolism appear to have some connection to suicide attempts (as well as other forms of impulsivity). Low levels of a serotonin metabolite called 5-HIAA in the cerebrospinal fluid have also been associated with increased rates of suicide.

PSYCHOLOGICAL AND SOCIAL FACTORS

I have discounted the importance of unhappy psychological events in a youngster's life as a cause for suicide by themselves, but this doesn't mean that no psychological factors are involved. There surely are, particularly for those who for other reasons are at high risk for suicide. Rage, passion, guilt, hopelessness, gloom, desperation—these are all real human emotions that play a role in a decision to attempt suicide, even if most people who experience these feelings never think of killing themselves. The urge, quite common among young suicide attempters, to use the threat of suicide as revenge or to arouse guilt or inspire pity—"You'll be sorry when I'm dead"—is a behavioral phenomenon, a psychological state of mind, not a mental illness.

So saying that psychiatric illness is the cause of suicide does not mean that treating and relieving the symptoms of the psychiatric illness will automatically eliminate the possibility of suicide. We can assert, correctly, that psychiatric illness represents the greatest risk for suicide, but there are emotional risks as well, unconnected to psychiatric illness. The motivations for suicide are complex, and they are modified by many factors, among them: religious beliefs, culture, family example, and the desire to influence others' emotions.

IN THEIR OWN WORDS: PARENTAL EXPECTATIONS, CULTURAL DIFFERENCES, THOUGHTS OF SUICIDE

I remember feeling kind of troubled in sixth grade, but I think it really started when I was in seventh grade and we moved to our new house. I felt very confused, not knowing how to fit in. Before that, I never had to deal with not being part of a group. Those feelings combined with moving. . . .

There was stuff going on inside my head, too. I think some of it has to do with cultural differences. My parents are from China so I was growing up in a Chinese household in the United States. My parents—their values were different from my peers, what I saw on TV. What my parents expected was really different from what I saw going on at parties and stuff.

I never thought about my mood as something I could do something about until ninth grade. I remember very distinctly deciding that I had to talk to someone. I went into the guidance counselor's office and almost before I could say anything, he said he wanted to make an appointment with someone for me to talk to. I remember smiling inside and thinking I was already ahead of the game.

I think I concealed it from my friends, held it in, tried to be more composed and calm. It's also a cultural thing. Talking about personal issues isn't a normal thing to do in Asian cultures. Your parents have expectations. You meet them. You follow their example. There's always a guide, someone looking, someone watching to make sure you do things the right way.

I never had any trouble falling asleep or staying asleep all night, but I'd wake up at six A.M. and feel really groggy. I had a kind of daily ebb and flow. When I awoke, I was neutral. School was routine. I like school, and I enjoyed meeting new friends. But it was always a mixed feeling because I would feel bad about myself, about my work. I couldn't do my work as well as I wanted to, and I would get angry at myself. And angry at everyone else, because I knew I was smarter than a lot of people who were doing better than me.

It was a relief to get home, go in my room, close the door, and just listen to music. I'd listen to music for three hours, just sitting in a chair and staring at the wall. I would just follow my thoughts.

At times, it was very dark, very sad. I felt I couldn't get up to do something physical. I felt utterly stuck. I thought about suicide a lot, even though it never came to the point of actually planning something. I just had fantasies. And I cut myself a couple of times.

I remember we went on a class trip—ten days away from home. In the middle of the trip, the fifth or sixth day, I tore up a soda can and cut myself accidentally. And I thought, now this is interesting, watching the blood well up on my hand. My friend was reading a book, and he looked up and saw my hand, and just freaked out. He went and got a teacher, and they had to tell my parents. There were a couple of other times I tried cutting myself, at home, just to see if I could get into that trancelike state.

In eleventh grade, I started taking Zoloft, and I think it really helped. Also, the psychiatrist was Chinese, and I felt he understood my complaints. Talking to someone definitely helped address the vague confusion I was feeling. Defining things, getting them out there under the lights, then filing them away. That was helpful.

After high school I started taking premed courses in college. I felt I should be a doctor because my parents wanted me to be one. But then after my second year in med school, I dropped out. I thought, this is my life, I have to do what I want. During that time at school, I saw a woman psychologist, an African-American woman. I don't know if that was helpful—but I guess it was, because I left med school. That was huge.

I'm seeing a psychologist now, a person who is very directive, which is what I need. Gradually I'm growing, feeling less stuck, feeling like I'm moving along, going someplace.

An experience like depression . . . it shows you you're not bullet-proof. Depression for me was a whole lot of apathy. There were days when I didn't care about anything. The worst part was—well, I'm more intellectual than emotional, and not being able to do anything with my mind was really bad. I felt I was not growing at all. I was stagnating, and it was really unbearable. It made me want to scream.

—Paul, age 25

Freud proposed that suicide was a homicide turned inward, an expression of hostility toward a lost love object, severe anger turned back against the self. In this formulation, suicide is the result of an unconscious desire to kill someone else. Although most experts now believe that these kinds of personality factors are not associated, or only weakly associated, with suicide, psychology is still useful in discovering and understanding the motivations for suicide, and it is certainly essential in counseling suicide attempters.

ROMANCE, REVENGE, AND SUICIDE

Occasionally a teenager will be brought into the emergency room because of a suicide attempt in the midst of a fight with a boyfriend. I first met Karen, a high school junior, after she had taken a bottle of Tylenol while on the phone with her boyfriend, Tommy, whom she learned was cheating on her. After she hung up on him, she called one of her friends and told her what she had done. The friend fortunately told her mother, who told Karen's parents, who called an ambulance.

Karen was much more concerned about breaking up with her

boyfriend than she was with the potential lethality of her suicide attempt. She thought taking Tylenol was "no big deal" (it is—swallowing a bottle of Tylenol can be fatal), but felt that she couldn't live without her boyfriend. It had always been an intense relationship, ever since ninth grade, and Karen remained very dependent on Tommy. When she learned of his infidelity, she felt her whole world was collapsing, and "just wanted to die." Once in the emergency room, and subsequently admitted to intensive care for treatment to prevent liver failure, she told me she really hadn't planned on taking an overdose, but that she was so hurt and angry that she wanted to punish Tommy for betraying her.

There are several more or less controversial psychological theories about the risk for suicide. Some feel that poor maternal bonding in early infancy may be a risk factor. Others have proposed that people who commit suicide have difficulty turning to others in times of need, and therefore turn on themselves. It is probably true that the loss of a parent in childhood (by death, divorce, or other cause) increases risk for both depression and suicide, and the separation of a teenager from someone important in his or her life also increases risk.

Some theorize that feelings of rage and experiences of violence contribute to motivation for suicide. Sometimes a youngster who is suicidal has a parent who has been violent or self-destructive; a severely disturbed youngster may have homicidal impulses as well as suicidal. People who kill others have a suicide rate several hundred times as high as those who do not, a rate largely the result of murder followed by suicide. Probably between 10 and 20 percent of suicide victims have had some history of other kinds of violent behavior.

Exposure to violence, either as a victim or observer, may cause an increase in stress that leads to suicidal behavior. At least one researcher noticed that black teenage suicides often occur in families where the mother or father has been physically abusive. Exposure to high levels of community violence has also been suggested as a cause of suicidal behavior. Coming from a broken home, having a mother with a mood disorder, or having a father who has had trouble with the police are all family phenomena that have been shown to increase risk for suicide.

Rage may be the most spectacular and obvious psychological state of a suicide attempter, but it is not the only one. Hopelessness and despair also characterize those who attempt to kill themselves. There is evidence that the severity of depression is less important in predicting whether a person will attempt suicide than whether the depression is dominated by feelings of hopelessness about the future. Where the youngster is not resigned to these feelings—that is, where the feelings are combined with a sense that life cannot continue without some change—suicide may be even more likely. Excessive or inappropriate feelings of guilt are a symptom of major depression, and when the feelings of guilt are so out of proportion that they are completely irrational or delusional, depressed youngsters are more likely to kill themselves.

Some teenagers give meaning to their desire to commit suicide. It becomes in their minds a "rebirth" in a better world; revenge or retaliation against parents, friends, or teachers; atonement for past sins. In suicidal teenagers, the feeling of being abandoned by parents or other loved ones is common, even when others may see no reason at all why the youngster would feel this way. Sometimes a teenager will feel that suicide is the only way he can gain control over events that seem otherwise uncontrollable. "I'll kill myself if I don't get into this college. . . ."

THE MAJOR RISK FACTORS

In high-risk patients—that is, patients who have threatened or attempted suicide—there are four risk factors that, taken together, account for more than 80 percent of the risk for suicide: major depression, bipolar disorder, a lack of previous mental health treatment, and the availability of firearms in the home. If these four problems were solved, most suicides would be prevented. The solutions are not totally out of reach.

Motivations for suicide vary with the culture: in some cultures psychological and social factors play a much greater role than they do for American teenagers. In certain Japanese settings, for example, suicide may be seen as an act of penance for bringing shame on the family, a socially acceptable, even honorable decision perfectly consonant with societal norms. In other cultural settings, suicide may be just the opposite: behavior completely outside social norms, representing a weakening of societal control over the individual.

Some have suggested that this weakening of societal control—the feeling on the part of the individual that the society has nothing to offer him—may be part of the explanation for the radical increases in suicide among black male teenagers. It is possible that this anomie leads to suicidal behavior. The high rates of suicide among elderly white men may result from exactly the same kind of feeling.

Among teenagers, both girls and boys, major depression increases the risk of suicide twelve-fold. A previous suicide attempt by a girl triples the likelihood that she will commit suicide. But a previous suicide attempt by a boy increases the likelihood that he will commit suicide more than thirty times. If a boy engages in disruptive behavior or drug abuse, these activities double his risk for suicide.

WHEN A SUICIDE ATTEMPT LOOKS LIKE AN ACCIDENT

I work in a community hospital. Every time there is an overdose in our emergency room, even if it looks like an accident, a psychiatrist is called in for an evaluation. That is how I came to meet George. He was 19, recently returned from a stay in a long-term drug rehabilitation facility. He was attending a community college now and living with his father—on the condition that he stay away from drugs. He didn't want to go back to rehab, and he'd been living up to his end of the bargain until he met some friends from the old days and started getting high again. Within a few weeks, he was back to using as often as he could, all the while pretending to his father that he was simply going to classes and carrying on normally. One Friday night, he decided that he could no longer face the inevitable—being thrown out of the house and being sent back to rehab. So he put together what he thought was enough heroin to kill himself and proceeded to use it. His friends, panicking when he passed out, brought him to the emergency room. He told the doctors what seemed a plausible story for a kid who'd recently come out of rehab: he was just trying to get high and took a little too much. It was only when I spent some time with him that he admitted that what he had really been trying to do was kill himself.

SCHOOL PROGRAMS FOR SUICIDE PREVENTION

Because suicide among adolescents, particularly among boys, has increased over the past several decades, many schools have instituted suicide prevention programs. Suicide clusters or copycat suicides are often the motivation for the creation of these programs. Parents and school officials generally attribute the sudden cluster of suicides to unlikely causes: an "insensitive" school administration, working mothers, latchkey children, even increases in the immigrant population in the community—all stresses (if you want to call them that) that have been present for a long period of time and couldn't possibly explain a sudden increase in suicide among teenagers. It is often in these periods of crisis and with these erroneous ideas in mind that suicide prevention programs are developed and implemented.

Generally speaking, school suicide prevention programs are run by school psychologists or outside mental health professionals. Some use "peer counselors," and sometimes the peer counselors are previously suicidal students. The programs are usually directed at students in the ninth grade or older and last about three hours. Sometimes they are directed only at teachers, who are expected to pass on their knowledge to their students. Most prevention programs have similar goals. They attempt to heighten awareness of the problem, often by showing videotapes of teenagers who have attempted suicide or by quoting statistics about suicide rates. They teach listening skills and describe warning signs of suicide (see box on pages 73–74). Often they attempt to elicit disclosure of suicidal thoughts by describing suicide in a way that will not stigmatize it— it is presented as a response to ordinary adolescent stress, pressure to succeed, family difficulties, and so on, instead of a sign of mental illness. They provide information about available mental health services. And some programs attempt to improve students' coping strategies or support students who have drug or alcohol problems, family problems, or failing grades.

Several studies have been done on the effectiveness of these programs in preventing suicide, and all are in agreement: they don't work. There are many reasons for this. First, suicide is uncommon. If you have a program that addresses all teenagers, as most school programs do, including the great majority who will never attempt suicide, its effectiveness is bound to be limited. It would probably be more effective to seek out teenagers at risk and direct programs at them, but this is much more difficult than designing a program that treats all teenagers alike.

Few kids are aware either before or after undergoing such programs that suicide is a feature of mental illness, not a normal response to stress. Anyone who presents it as anything other than a symptom of mental illness is either ignorant or, however well intentioned, distorting the truth. Moreover, it may be that presenting suicide as if it were a normal response to adolescent life's many stresses may inadvertently encourage it. If we want to make suicide a less attractive option, it seems to me that it would make a lot more sense to present it as what it is: a pathological act by a person with a mental illness who needs emergency medical treatment. Often the prevention programs include filmed vignettes of suicidal behavior or interviews with suicide attempters or survivors. There is considerable question whether this has the opposite effect, encouraging the "copycat" phenomenon described above.

School programs may be effective in screening out some teenagers who are suicidal and who want professional help, and to the extent that they are, they could be useful. It must be remembered that it is much harder to convince boys to go for treatment than girls. This may be because boys believe it's wimpy to go and talk about their problems, that a real man should be able to handle it himself. But every community knows of some bright college boy who comes home for a school break and kills himself for no apparent reason. In any case, it would be a much better use of resources to concentrate on the kids who are likely to attempt suicide, and treat them with the proven techniques of modern clinical psychiatry described elsewhere in this book. Most teenagers don't need school suicide prevention programs; those who do will find little benefit in them. Teachers and school administrators should always be acutely aware of the possibility that there may be a suicidal teenager under their supervision, but these programs are not a good way of identifying those kids.

TELEPHONE HOTLINES

Suicide crisis services are usually run by telephone. They are available at all hours, and offer callers someone to talk to whenever necessary. Their anonymity and convenience may appeal to teenagers who would be much less likely to use conventional mental health services—only a small percentage of callers to hotlines has ever been in treatment. Most centers are organized and advertised locally, but there are some national hotlines as well—the National Adolescent Runaway/Suicide Hotline is one. Hotlines are usually staffed by volunteers, sometimes teenagers, who are trained and supervised by mental health professionals.

Few of these hotlines offer direct therapy. Most offer a sympathetic ear to confide in and then referral to a mental health facility. Some hotlines follow up to see that appointments are kept, and most will break confidentiality by calling the police if they sense that there is a reason to do so. Usually they ask permission before calling a teenager's parents.

Hotlines are much appreciated by those who use them, and they may have some limited effect in reducing suicide rates, but they fall short for various reasons. Awareness of the existence of a hotline is far from universal among teenagers, even where they are advertised. Training and competency of the hotline operators varies considerably, and some hand out bad advice—hasty, prejudiced, or based on ignorance. Outreach—making appointments for callers and following up on them—varies considerably, and where it is poor, the hotline is much less effective. Still, a hotline, if it is properly run, supervised, and evaluated, can be helpful to a teenager in trouble.

RESTRICTING ACCESS TO METHODS FOR COMMITTING SUICIDE

In 1957, when the carbon monoxide content of domestic coal gas supplies was 12 percent, self-asphyxiation with gas accounted for more than 40 percent of British suicides. By 1970, natural gas had been introduced with a carbon monoxide content of only 2 percent—and was much harder to kill yourself with. Over the period of introduction of the new gas, suicides by gas declined steadily until they accounted for less than 10 percent of all suicides—and the total suicide rate had also gone down by 26 percent. That is, there was no compensatory increase in suicides by other means. The elimination of a convenient and effective means of committing suicide actually reduced the suicide rate, and did so significantly.

Certain locations are magnets for suicide attempters. The Golden Gate Bridge in San Francisco was one until authorities constructed barriers that now prevent people from jumping, efficiently restricting access to that means of suicide.

Teenage suicide is often an impulsive act, so eliminating the easiest means to make a suicide attempt would reduce suicide rates. The fact is that a majority of adolescents who try to kill themselves and do not succeed don't try it again (although, as we will see below, about 40 percent do). Removing the means for a single impulsive act might substantially cut down on successful suicide. In the United States, most teenage suicides occur by gunfire (see box on page 69). Guns are always an extremely effective means of committing suicide, and in many instances they are conveniently available. The connection between gun availability and adolescent suicide rates can be proven in many ways: the rate of firearms suicide is directly proportional to the number of guns made, sold, and owned; suicide by gun is significantly less common in local areas with strict gun control laws than in those without; the effect of reducing access to guns is much more significant in reducing adolescent suicide rates than in reducing adult suicide rates. The doubling of the adolescent suicide rate in the past three decades is largely accounted for by the increase in suicide by gun. Eliminating teenagers' access to guns would almost certainly reduce their suicide rate.

TALKING TO A SUICIDAL TEENAGER

Most adolescents who contemplate suicide think that there is no one to help them with their problems, and that they must solve them alone—half don't even bother to ask for help before attempting to harm themselves. Thinking about death and suicide is fairly common among high-schoolers, so common that it is probably not a reliable way of estimating actual risk, but overt statements from a teenager such as "I want to kill myself" or threats like "I'm going to commit suicide" must be taken seriously, and parents must immediately seek professional help. Although it may be uncomfortable to do it, talking about the problem with the teenager is important, too. Some feel that asking a youngster whether she is thinking about suicide will "put ideas into her head," but in fact such discussions can be extremely helpful, providing someone to talk to and assurances that someone cares. Given the opportunity, suicidal adolescents are often not reluctant to talk, and they can be highly reliable reporters of their suicidal potential, especially if asked in nonthreatening ways. Direct questions are best: Have you thought about harming yourself? Have you tried to hurt yourself in the past? Do you know anyone who tried to commit suicide? How did it make you feel? When I ask questions like this—and listen carefully to the answers—I usually get the truth. Any parent or friend can do the same.

TREATMENT OF SUICIDAL TEENAGERS

Psychiatric treatment can't prevent all suicides, but it is the best tool we have. Though most kids who commit suicide have evidence of a psychiatric disorder, only about half have ever had the attention of a mental health professional. One effective prevention technique, although it hasn't been widely studied, would be to provide mental health services on-site in schools to catch suicides before they happen. Depression, conduct disorder, and alcohol and drug abuse are all major risk factors for suicide, and they are all treatable illnesses if they are diagnosed in time.

I want to emphasize that the presence of psychiatric illness is by any measure the largest risk factor for suicide. The most common diagnoses are a mood disorder alone or a mood disorder in combination with substance abuse or conduct disorder. In one large study, alcohol or substance abuse was more common among male suicides and mood disorders more common among female. Less than half of the suicides had had any contact at all with a mental health professional. Under 10 percent of suicide victims appeared to be free of any psychiatric symptoms before death.

All this means that psychiatric treatment of teenagers who threaten or attempt suicide is our one best hope. The precise details of what kind of treatment is the most effective are still the subject of study and debate, but much is known that can give parents and teenagers reason for optimism even when matters seem to be at their worst. Since depression is by far the most common illness in suicidal kids, I always try first to find out if this is part of the problem. If it is, medication becomes a critical part of the treatment.

Kids who attempt suicide, unless they are so injured that they are medically hospitalized, wind up in a psychiatric emergency room (see box below). What happens to them there can have a significant effect on their subsequent treatment. Depending on the situation, psychiatric hospitalization (see chapter 9) or outpatient treatment may be the next step.

THE PSYCHIATRIC EMERGENCY ROOM

Psychiatric emergency rooms (ER) vary, depending on the hospital. Freestanding psychiatric hospitals have an evaluation area, usually an office, with a psychiatrist or a social worker who interviews patients. Community hospitals usually don't have a separate psychiatric ER, but a designated area in the general emergency room used for psychiatric emergencies. Here you are likely to see medical patients in an open area, but a discussion with a psychiatrist takes place in a private room. In a large hospital, a psychiatric ER can be more intimidating. There may be people waiting who are clearly agitated, sometimes accompanied by police or other security personnel. This is not to say that the ER is a dangerous place. Everyone in it is trained to deal with crises, and the safety of the patients is paramount. For the most part, even these ERs, crowded and hectic though they may be, are not too different from waiting in a doctor's office.

If a youngster is released from the hospital, she should be given an appointment to see a therapist. Often, kids don't want to keep these appointments. Should a parent accept this? After all, the adolescent is feeling well again, the crisis seems past, she's no longer feeling suicidal. Maybe it's best at this point to let sleeping dogs lie.

This course of action—and there is no gentler way to state it—can be fatal. In fact, the teenagers most likely to complete a suicide are also the most likely to fail to keep psychiatric appointments. Recurrence of suicidal behavior in adolescents who have been treated is high: up to 40 percent of recovered suicide attempters will try it again within two years. It is absolutely essential to impress upon the youngster the importance of following up with psychiatric care, even compelling it when necessary. (I'll have more to say about compelling kids into treatment in chapter 10.)

Although you don't have much choice of which doctor or other professional you're going to see when you go to an emergency room, that person's clinical skills are extremely important in assuring a successful outcome. Some clinicians are much better able to persuade youngsters to seek continuing care than others are.

If you come into a hospital ER and you see security present in the form of uniformed guards or other security people, that's a good sign. As soon as a kid comes into an emergency room because of a suicide attempt, security should be watching him. Often teenagers run out and disappear—the worst possible outcome in this situation. If you come into an emergency room that isn't equipped in this way, you have to make sure that your youngster doesn't leave. If saying "My kid just tried suicide" doesn't result in someone being called to guard him in some way, you have to be ready to guard him yourself. I had one boy who ran out of the emergency room, jumped in his father's Range Rover, and drove right through the parking lot barrier.

Most parents are completely overwhelmed the first time they bring their teenager into an emergency room. They're terrified for the youngster's physical health, and shocked by what he has done to himself: they had no idea this was going on. Often they feel helpless and just take direction from whoever sees the teenager first. Both parent and child are in crisis, and I try to be as clear as possible at the outset. What has happened here is significant, even if it looks like the teenager is going to be physically OK, and we need to figure out the best way to treat this.

Obviously, if an adolescent has injured herself, the emergent medical situation is the first thing that has to be treated. Any type of overdose has to be immediately evaluated and treated. Some seemingly innocuous medicines such as aspirin and Tylenol can be lethal in large enough doses. So all overdoses require attention, even if the youngster is alert. Time is of the essence. Medical staff may give agents that induce vomiting, or they may administer antidotes, depending on the substance ingested.

If there is any chance of medical complications, the patient must be hospitalized, usually in the intensive care unit, for close monitoring for the first 24 hours after the incident. But even where there is no obvious physical injury, medical workups are important. There are numerous medical illnesses, including acute intoxication, that can cause depression and suicidal impulses (see chapter 5). You need a medical doctor to make these determinations.

The standard procedure in the emergency room is first to stabilize the patient. This requires that the emergency room physician perform a medical evaluation and treat accordingly. The psychiatrist is called once the patient is medically stable or is able to communicate, even if he or she is still undergoing evaluation or treatment.

Empathy is essential. These teenagers are scared. They've done something about which they often feel guilty or at least chagrined. Sometimes they're angry—often as a defense against those other emotions.

Usually, I want to talk to the adolescent first. I try to make this an open-ended discussion because I want to hear what the kid is going to say—I want to hear him talk. If he seems hesitant, I say something like this: "I know you don't want to be here, but if you don't talk to me, I don't have any choice except to hospitalize you. The best thing you can do is tell me what you're thinking and what you've been doing so that we can make the best decision." If after I've used whatever persuasive skills I have, the youngster still refuses to talk, he gets admitted to the hospital. We'll discuss it when he's ready, but he's not going home without my gaining some understanding of what has happened. (See chapter 9 for a discussion of voluntary and involuntary treatment, how inpatient treatment is insured, and other issues in psychiatric hospitalization.)

Sometimes I'll see the parents first to get some background. "Tell me what I'm missing here before I sit down with your child." Then I go in and talk to the child. If I feel that hospitalization is necessary, I tell the teenager first. Then I tell the parents what I've told the youngster. I don't leave it to the parents to tell the teenager what has to be done. The psychiatrist has to have the courage of her convictions, be firm, and take charge.

When I tell the parents what the situation is, their agreement is almost always forthcoming. After all, they've seen how serious the situation is or they wouldn't have brought the adolescent to the emergency room in the first place. The usual reaction from parents is relief that someone is taking care of the problem. They are generally in no mood to argue.

In an emergency room, the possibility of hospitalization is fairly clear from the start, but hospitalizing a kid from a private office is a little more problematic. Sometimes I'll be talking with a young patient in my office when I discover that suicide is a real possibility. It is likely that what follows will be something like this: "What you're telling me is very serious, and, because you're feeling the way you are, you can't go home. It wouldn't be safe. I want you to stay here, and we're going to call someone to get you over to the hospital. I'm going to stay here with you until we can arrange some transportation." This may spring things on them, which isn't a good idea, but sometimes it's unavoidable. At the beginning of treatment with a teenager, I make it clear that everything they say is confidential, except information that I think is life-threatening.

Some parents say they're afraid to take the teenager home. This is an opinion that has to be respected, even if the kid says there's nothing to worry about. It's always better to get a youngster into the hospital, even if only for 24 to 48 hours of observation, than to leave her in a doubtful situation.

Some ERs have mental health professionals who screen patients, then call the doctor and present the case to the doctor. The doctor then makes a decision via a phone call. This happens particularly in rural areas where there is shortage of psychiatrists. But if it's serious enough to get you to an emergency room, you should insist on seeing a doctor. Demands like this don't win popularity contests among emergency room staff, but you're not there to win one. You're there to see that your teenager gets the best care possible.

Sometimes a parent will refuse to hospitalize a child. Often divorced parents argue over what should be done, one parent trying to be the good guy by saying, "You're OK. I'll take care of you." I tell them I'm sorry, but in my judgment—and it's my judgment that's going to prevail here—he needs to be hospitalized. I'd rather be sued than let a kid go whom I think is in danger of committing suicide. I explain to the parents that, legally, I can keep a person for observation for up to 72 hours, with other psychiatrists evaluating the patient at 24 hours and again at 48 hours. (This is the law in New York. The details of the laws vary considerably from state to state, but every state has regulations allowing people to be kept against their will in certain circumstances.) I'm not talking about a locked ward, or shutting someone up in a "nuthouse." I'm talking about a standard of medical care to which everyone is entitled.

Not all suicide attempts end in hospitalization. Sometimes it isn't necessary. If a kid makes a nonlethal attempt in front of her parents—in other words, if it's clear that this is a gesture and not a serious attempt—then hospitalization may not be necessary. There are some situations where direct interventions in the emergency room will defuse a situation enough so that outpatient treatment will suffice. But even here, each case is different.

I consider some indications reason for automatic hospitalization no matter what else is happening: if a teenage suicide attempter is abusing substances, or if he's used (or planned to use) a deadly weapon in the attempt, the reason doesn't matter—he'll get hospitalized.

If I send someone home, I impose certain conditions. I never send anyone home alone without support, so there has to be a responsible adult available. There must be a plan in place for seeking appropriate treatment. And there has to be good reason for me to believe that everyone, parents and child alike, will be determined to follow through on the plan. Teen suicide attempters who keep appointments with mental health professionals are much less likely to try it again than those who don't, no matter how serious their attempt was or how serious their medical injury.

Usually, both the teenager and her parents understand the reasons why hospitalization is necessary. The parents, and the psychiatrist, have to be the child's advocate in these situations.

PARENTS IN DENIAL

Parents can be extremely reluctant to acknowledge mental illness in their teenage children and are often willing, despite ample evidence to the contrary, to deny the seriousness of depression in a teenager. Thirteen-year-old Mark was the youngest of four children, and all the others were doing well in high school or at Ivy League colleges. His parents, concerned that their youngest was spending too much time playing with friends, began imposing certain rules. He was not allowed out of the house until all his schoolwork and chores were done to the satisfaction of his father, a rather stern taskmaster, and the rule was enforced without mercy.

In a fairly well-thought-out plan, Mark had begun hoarding pills that he thought would be lethal, and one night he took them with a bottle of vodka while his parents were attending a school function for his brother. That evening they found him passed out with a number of empty pill bottles next to him, and they called an ambulance. He was admitted to the intensive care unit at our hospital.

Within several hours, his siblings and parents were in the room with him, reassuring him and telling him how much they cared. Over the next few days, during which he stayed in the ICU because of a cardiac arrhythmia, his family never left his side. When he stabilized, they initially agreed to have him transferred to a psychiatric unit, but almost from the day of his arrival there they began pressing for his discharge. They didn't think he belonged in a psychiatry unit, he wasn't that sick, certainly not as disturbed as the other patients they saw there. And anyway, they planned to back off, not put so much pressure on him, so why couldn't he just come home?

Clearly they couldn't imagine their son as someone in need of psychiatric treatment, but since he was no longer suicidal, I had no reason to hold him in the hospital—even though intensive treatment for his depression would certainly have been a good idea.

PSYCHOLOGICAL TREATMENT

The first-line treatment for suicidal teenagers is hospitalization and medication for the underlying disorder. But psychological treatment combined with these therapies is important as well. For a psychiatrist, suicidal patients are perhaps the most difficult. They are, after all, their only patients who are in imminent danger of dying. Teenagers (and other suicidal people) may become angry and blame those closest to them for their problems, or they may try to use threats of suicide as a means of manipulation, so the therapist can easily become the object of this hatred and manipulation. Of course, the therapist must be aware that he or she is neither the savior nor the executioner, and the ways in which the therapist reacts to threats and manipulation will be critical to successful treatment. Teenagers, like other people, sometimes lie—they say they're fine but they still have in mind a plan to commit suicide. Seeing through such a lie can be difficult; failing to see through it can be tragic. It takes considerable understanding, profound knowledge, and much experience to treat such patients effectively.

In most psychiatric treatment, medication and psychotherapy are more effective than either alone, and this is true of suicidal patients as well. Even with the same severity of depressive symptoms, some kids will attempt suicide and some won't. So clearly there is a psychology to the decision as well, and paying attention to psychological motivations is critical. A therapist who understands both the biological and psychological causes of suicidal impulses is the one most likely to be successful.

We've listed warning signs that a kid may attempt suicide (see box, pages 73–74), but this doesn't mean that suicide or suicide attempts are easily predictable. They aren't—not even by experienced mental health professionals.

5

Depression and Other Teenage Problems

Kids who are depressed are significantly at risk for other problems, both physical and psychiatric—what physicians call "comorbidity." Depression is highly associated with eating disorders, anxiety disorders, personality disturbances, and substance abuse. The relationships between these disorders—aside from the observation that they often occur together—is unclear. Does depression cause these other disorders? Do the other disorders cause depression? Or is there some other thing that causes both depression and the other disorders? No one knows for sure, but I do know that depressed teenagers I see often come in with a host of other problems as well.

There are some physical diseases that cause depression (particularly endocrine disorders such as thyroid disease or any illness that raises levels of steroids in the body such as Cushing's syndrome), and in these cases the depression should be treated just as aggressively as the physical illness itself. Sometimes depression leads to other problems—one example of this is kids who treat themselves for depression by smoking cigarettes. Moreover, depression in adolescence is associated with future problems, particularly with increased episodes and increased severity of depression in adult life, but also with other psychiatric and medical problems.

CIGARETTE SMOKING

Adolescents, as any parent knows, are at considerable risk for abusing drugs, both legal and illegal. Most doctors would agree with me that the drug that does the most harm to the greatest number of teenagers is nicotine. Smoking almost always begins in adolescence, and this is why nicotine addiction is now viewed by many experts as a pediatric disease. If kids reach the age of 19 without taking up smoking, it is unlikely that they ever will. Why do kids smoke? Well, of course all their friends are doing it, and it looks cool, and these are powerful reasons. But there may be another reason that is just as compelling: nicotine helps counter the symptoms of depression.

STARTING SMOKING DURING A DEPRESSIVE EPISODE

Lily had been treated for depression in high school, quite successfully, with Zoloft. It had helped her through a difficult time with her parents and teachers, and she continued on the medicine into her freshman year at college. But her symptoms—severe crying spells as well as panic attacks—returned. When I increased her dose, she developed severe headaches, a common side effect, and shaking, a less common one. Over a period of several months, I switched her to Paxil, and finally to Luvox, but during this time she began smoking. By the time we had found the correct medicine and dosage, she was smoking a half a pack a day, and though she tried to quit, she found it impossible.

Researchers have studied this phenomenon. One study examined a group of high school students when they were 15 and 16, and then interviewed the same students when they were 24 and 25 years old.

The adolescents who had suffered from depression were much more likely to be smokers than those who had not. Major depression is a significant risk factor for the onset of smoking, and the risk is just as great for boys as for girls. There is even evidence that the severity of depression can be directly correlated with the number of cigarettes a teenager smokes. Smoking is not, apparently, associated with other psychiatric disorders; for example, the researchers found no increased smoking among youngsters with anxiety disorder. (An exception is schizophrenia: almost 90 percent of people with this diagnosis also smoke.)

It is more difficult for girls to quit smoking than for boys, a difference that persists into adulthood. So if a teenage girl is smoking, it is all the more important to find out if she is depressed, and, if she is, to treat the illness. One parent I know, recently diagnosed with breast cancer, reported that her daughter began smoking more as soon as she learned of her mother's diagnosis.

Two-thirds of kids who smoke also suffer from a psychiatric illness. So smoking itself is a warning sign that other problems may require attention. This also means that smoking prevention efforts should take into account the existence of other problems, especially major depression. Trying to get any adolescent to quit smoking is very difficult. If I try telling a kid that smoking causes lung cancer and dozens of other serious diseases, it makes almost no impression at all. Kids just don't think that way, and prevention programs that concentrate on getting adolescents to understand the health dangers of smoking are largely ineffective. Those that emphasize social skills and resistance to peer pressure work a little better. But since depression is so closely associated with taking up the habit, finding the depressed, or otherwise psychiatrically ill, young smokers and getting psychiatric treatment for them may turn out to be the most effective anti-smoking program of all. Since smoking is associated with marijuana and other illegal substance use, this kind of initiative may even reduce the abuse of those drugs as well.

ALCOHOL ABUSE

Alcohol is another drug commonly abused by adolescents, and combined with driving automobiles or other risky physical activities it can be fatal. In the kind of suburban area where I practice, alcohol-related car accidents are probably the single largest cause of teenage death. In kids who are depressed abusing alcohol complicates mood disorders and increases the risk of suicide. About 5 percent of adolescents can actually be classified as alcoholics. Almost all adolescents who abuse alcohol have another psychiatric disorder as well; studies have found that somewhere between one-third and one-half of kids who abuse alcohol also suffer from a mood disorder, most commonly major depression and dysthymia.

It is easy to ignore the presence of mood disorders in teenagers who abuse alcohol—these youngsters are misbehaving, and it is the misbehavior that gets the most attention, for good and obvious reasons. But behind the behavior quite often is depression, and it is important to treat the depression as well as the behavior problems. In fact, treating the depression may well help in controlling the alcohol abuse.

Alcohol and depression, like smoking and depression, may be a two-way street. There is some evidence that abusing alcohol can cause depression, and some studies have shown that abstinent alcoholics have lower rates of depression than those who are still drinking. For this reason and others, I prefer to have a youngster stop drinking before treatment for depression begins, but continuing use is not a reason to delay treatment for depression. Sometimes I have an adolescent who deliberately comes to a session high, trying, usually, to see what kind of reaction she'll get out of me, to see if she'll be criticized or judged. I don't refuse to treat such kids, but I do try to determine what they're trying to tell me by coming to a session impaired.

If a kid is abusing alcohol, she has to be in a program that will address the alcohol abuse as well as the depression. Drinking in combination with antidepressants isn't a good idea, and alcohol is itself a depressant. Dual diagnosis programs are the solution in these cases, and both problems must be treated simultaneously.

TRAUMATIC INJURY

Adolescents, especially boys, take risks and get serious physical injuries. Motor vehicle injuries are by far the most common physically disabling injuries teenagers suffer, but other accidents and sports injuries are also frequent. When these injuries are serious enough, a youngster can seem depressed. Physical injury, like any medical illness, is a risk factor for depression. But there is a difference between depression, which may last months or years, and normal grief or rage after a disabling injury. Untreated depression in these circumstances is associated with lower rates of recovery, noncompliance with treatment, and increased withdrawal and isolation.

It's too easy to say, "Of course he's depressed—he's confined to a wheelchair." While grief is a perfectly normal response to such a severe disability, no one should assume that being confined to a wheelchair in itself causes clinical depression, or that recovery from a physical injury will relieve the depression. Nor is it true that the only way to cure the depression is to cure the physical illness or eliminate the disability.

In many ways, a physical illness is often more easily dealt with by family and friends than a psychological illness. There is an unfortunate tendency among people to believe that if a youngster is in a hospital for treatment of a broken neck, he's unlucky; but if he's there for treatment of depression, he's "nuts." It's important to remember that depression is a treatable illness, whatever its cause, and treating it makes physical recovery much easier.

AN ACCIDENT LEADS TO DEPRESSION

Fred was 16, a well-adjusted, bright, athletic high school sopho-more, when a car he was riding in smashed head-on into a pickup truck driving in the other direction. The accident left him in a coma with signs of such severe neurological injury that doctors thought he'd never recover. But after seventeen days, he woke up. During the next two months, with continuing physical therapy, he made remarkable progress toward recovery. Physically, he was doing extremely well, but the injury had left him with some cognitive impairment and difficulty controlling his emotions. Other kids in the car were injured, too, and their recovery was not as successful as his, which made him feel guilty.

Once a well-liked kid, he became withdrawn and antisocial. Physical problems continued to plague him as well. His coordina-tion wasn't as good as it used to be, and he had to give up sports. He almost had a physical altercation with a former coach, and the inci-dent got him suspended from school.

After that incident, he decided to "borrow" his parents' car and leave town. When his parents tried to stop him, he threatened to kill himself. It was this threat that brought him to the hospital and into my office.

Fred's parents had noticed his behavior—there was no way to miss it—but they thought it would get better by itself, just as his physical injuries had largely healed. But the psychological effects of his injury were not healing by themselves—indeed, over time they were getting worse. Neither Fred nor his parents wanted to stig-matize him with psychiatric illness in addition to his physical prob-lems, so they decided that the best thing to do was pretend there were no psychological problems. Obviously, this was not working.

I hospitalized Fred, as I would anyone who seriously threatens suicide. It is conceivable that the depression had an organic cause—that is, that the brain injury caused it. But there was no way to be sure. In any case, Fred needed both cognitive therapy to work on the symptoms of his brain injury, and medication to relieve his depression. He was very explosive, and his dramatic mood swings led to some aggressive behavior on the ward. But after two weeks he had calmed down on medication enough to be discharged, and we referred him to a neuropsychologist for cognitive treatment.

ANXIETY DISORDERS

Worry and anxiety are a normal part of teenage life (and of adult life, for that matter), but teenagers suffering from anxiety disorder as a psychiatric illness have acute symptoms that persist over a period of months and interfere with normal functioning. For example, any youngster might feel anxious about starting high school, but one with anxiety disorder may be unable to leave the house without overwhelming sensations of panic and multiple physical symptoms such as trouble breathing, rapid heartbeat, choking, nausea, and vomiting.

Many youngsters with depression also suffer from anxiety. A small group of patients actually suffer from "mixed anxiety depressive disorder," which is not yet a DSM-IV diagnosis but may turn out to be a disorder separate from both anxiety and depression. Anxiety and depression are now considered two separate diseases, which a teenager can suffer from simultaneously.

Anxiety disorders are common in depressed youngsters—the lifetime risk of major depression in people suffering from them is close to 40 percent. Anxiety complicates the treatment for depression: both are treated with antidepressant medications, but the drugs must be selected and prescribed differently when both illnesses are involved. Thus it is important to know whether anxiety accompanies the depression.

The spectrum of anxiety disorders ranges from quite mild worrying to severe forms like panic disorder and agoraphobia. School phobias are a common form of anxiety. A typical version of adolescent anxiety is the teenager who is an extreme perfectionist—she can't turn in a paper that has the least flaw, which results in an inability to turn in the paper at all. Substance abuse is often a result of anxiety, a form of self-treatment for the illness.

TOO PERFECT

Judy was a 17-year-old college freshman who had always wanted to be a scientist. Her parents recognized her abilities early on and encouraged her in her studies. In high school, her teachers began to comment on how upset she became over the slightest imperfection in her work. At home she would spend inordinate amounts of time on her homework, struggling to create perfect papers and projects. No matter how hard she worked and how many hours she put in, she felt unprepared.

Judy was accepted by a prestigious university with a full scholarship, but within the first few months of her freshman year she became completely overwhelmed with her studies. She couldn't be perfect at everything, no matter how hard she tried. There were other students who were brighter than she was, and she was constantly comparing herself to them. She stopped eating and stopped sleeping, and was finally sent home by the school to get treatment. During the course of my evaluation, it became apparent that she was suffering from severe anxiety related to fears of failure and an almost delusional sense of inadequacy. She needed antidepressants that treated both depression and severe obsessiveness. Initially she also required an antipsychotic medication to help contain the delusion that she was horribly stupid and would be found out by her professors. She also needed psychotherapy to address her long-term feelings that she was a "freak" and unlike the rest of her family.

Sometimes I'll treat a depression, and it doesn't get better because there's still an element of anxiety. The mood is good, but the anxiety remains. In such cases, I figure out what drugs have to be added to treat the anxiety.

BEHAVIOR PROBLEMS, CONDUCT DISORDER

This is a problem I discussed briefly in chapter 3, but it is important to consider in the context of this chapter as well. Some teenagers act up—staying out too late, failing to do their schoolwork, becoming rebellious, sullen, defiant, or dishonest with parents, teachers, and other authority figures. They try on different identities, often dressing or talking in ways that are clearly intended to shock. They can be impulsive—grabbing the keys to the car to take a drive when they know they shouldn't, taking physical risks that upon later reflection they realize were irrational. They test the boundaries of possible behaviors and attitudes as they solidify a sense of conscience and responsibility. All this helps to establish an identity as an adult separate from parents and teachers and is a normal task of adolescent development.

Conduct disorder, however, is something else entirely, and not just an extension of this kind of rather ordinary teenage limit-testing. The essential feature of the disorder is a persistent pattern of behavior that seriously violates societal norms or the rights of others. Vandalism and deliberate fire-setting are characteristic. Kids with conduct disorder are often bullies. They initiate physical fights and use weapons (a brick, a broken bottle, a knife, or a gun) to threaten or harm people. They have little concern for the feelings of others, blame others for their own misdeeds, see threats where there are none, and respond with what they believe to be justified aggression. These teenagers often steal, break into houses or cars, and sometimes mug people with the threat of force. They lie to obtain favors, break promises, and con people into getting their way. Guilt and remorse are foreign to them, self-esteem is low. Truancy and running away from home are also characteristic of the disorder.

Teenagers who are depressed are more likely to have a conduct disorder than those who are not. For example, it has been shown that the more depressed a youngster is in the ninth grade the more likely he or she is to be found carrying a handgun in twelfth grade. If we needed no other motivation to do so, this kind of information makes seeking out and helping depressed kids a matter of great urgency.

EATING DISORDERS

Eating disorders—bulimia and anorexia—are much more common in girls than in boys, but they are a fairly common psychiatric disorder of adolescence. More than 3 percent of teenage girls will suffer from one of these disorders. In anorexia, the youngster refuses to maintain a normal body weight, often dieting to the point of starvation with its attendant health problems, and has a severely distorted perception of her own body's appearance. Bulimia is characterized by alternate periods of binge eating and self-induced vomiting, with a similar distorted perception of body shape and weight. These disorders are often accompanied by other psychiatric disorders, most commonly by depression—as many as half of kids with eating disorders are also depressed and the two disorders may be linked genetically. Bipolar disorder (see pages 43–46) is also common among teenagers suffering from eating disorders.

IN THEIR OWN WORDS: BODY IMAGE

I can't stand taking a shower because I can't stand facing the reality of my body. I don't even mean its bulk or ugliness now, but simply its existence as a physical entity in its own right. I just don't want to deal with the confines of it, the weight of the task of carrying it around, taking it with me like a huge overstuffed bag that contains my organs and which I literally can't live without. The restrictions. . . . I want to be freed of it and all its dreadful connotations, including those of having it be alive and thinking and the subsequent dull gray discontent I drag around with it.

—Anna, age 16

Cause and effect are hard to establish, because depression is seen in people who are not anorexic but are undergoing starvation. In other words, the depression may be a physiological consequence of the lack of food. Or it may be a two-way street: depression leads to eating disorders, eating disorders aggravate depression. Prozac in high doses is used to treat bulimia, and treating anorexics with antidepressants for underlying mood symptoms is now standard. When I treat someone with an eating disorder, I always reassess the depression after normal weight is restored.

SELF-MUTILATION

Despite the analogy Julia makes in the box on page 108, self-mutilation bears no relationship to body piercing or tattooing. The act of deliberately cutting, chafing, or burning the skin is the disturbed behavior of a person suffering from a mental illness, not an attempt by a youngster to keep up with a fashion trend. It is a compulsion, not a decision thoughtfully arrived at and then deliberately carried out.

Self-mutilation has not been widely studied, and it is not even listed as a separate disorder in the DSM-IV, but rather as one of the diagnostic criteria of borderline personality disorder. Almost no peer-reviewed scientific studies of the phenomenon have been published; there are no accurate statistics on its frequency; and its causes remain obscure. We are left with clinical impressions rather than scientifically tested conclusions, and most of what is written about the phenomenon is based on the personal experience of therapists with teenagers who have engaged in the behavior.

It seems generally agreed that self-mutilation can be a feature of depression, particularly in adolescents, and that parents and therapists should be aware of the possibility of such behavior in depressed teenagers.

IN THEIR OWN WORDS: SELF-MUTILATION

I'm trying to hide the carefully scabbed slash marks on my ankle from my mom and dad for fear they'll hide all the kitchen knives like they did the last time I cut myself. I think that the cutting has been the hardest part of my depression for my parents for the simple reason that they don't understand. They come from a generation that did not self-mutilate, be it with tattoos, nipple rings, or intentional razorblade gashes. They just don't get it. It's so hard to rationalize pain. Cutting lets off pressure. Some days I must cut or I will explode, swelling up like a manic balloon. Self-abuse says what words cannot, goes beyond eloquence to gut feeling. To pain. To cut is to make a clean purge of the stories lurking directly beneath your skin. . . .

—Julia, age 14

ATTENTIONAL PROBLEMS AND HYPERACTIVITY

This disorder—officially called attention-deficit/hyperactivity disorder (ADHD)—is marked by an inability to concentrate or sit still, aggressive behavior, problems in schoolwork, clumsiness, and learning disabilities. The disorder begins in childhood, usually before the age of 7, and for the diagnosis to be made, the symptoms have to be severe enough to cause serious disruption in school or at home. Although it always begins in childhood, it can persist into adolescence, and sometimes the diagnosis isn't made until that time. Adults may still suffer from the illness. About 3 to 5 percent of children have this diagnosis, but there isn't sufficient data to establish the prevalence among adolescents.

It is now believed that at least some of the children who demonstrate these symptoms are depressed. Their low self-esteem and feelings of worthlessness are similar to those of depressed children. As many as 30 percent of children with ADHD may also be depressed.

Diagnosing ADHD is difficult and somewhat controversial, particularly in milder cases. Some feel the diagnosis is overused to control normally active youngsters for the convenience of teachers and parents rather than to help children with a true psychiatric disorder. But Ritalin and sometimes other medications clearly help some kids to concentrate better and exercise better social judgment. These drugs can be a valuable treatment.

Particularly where the treatment for ADHD is unsuccessful, depression may be the problem. It is always essential to check for an overactive thyroid gland, which can produce symptoms similar to this disorder.

SEXUAL IDENTITY

According to the U.S. Department of Health and Human Services, 30 percent of adolescent suicides are committed by kids who belong to a sexual minority, and suicide attempts among these youngsters are two to three times as common as among heterosexual teenagers.

This does not mean that being gay, lesbian, bisexual, or transgendered in itself makes adolescents more likely to be depressed. The problem more likely stems from the difficulties these teenagers often have in coming to terms with and expressing their sexuality. Such kids face all the problems any adolescent faces when it comes to sex—puzzlement, fear, embarrassment, shame, confusion—yet in addition they must deal with stigma, prejudice, social isolation, stereotyping, verbal insults, physical attacks, and more. These stresses may provoke depression, and any tendency toward depression may magnify stresses. It is important for parents to understand that sexual preferences are not voluntary, and that these teenagers do best when family members can accept their differences.

IS IT AN ILLNESS OR JUST WHO YOU ARE?

Some kids seem much more restrained than others, less likely to be the center of attention or the life of the party. They keep to themselves, don't interact much with the other kids, seem preoccupied with their own thoughts, stay quiet when others are making noise. They prefer to be left alone rather than engage in social interactions, and they may seem older or more mature than the others. They don't especially like parties or other social occasions, and are not part of any significant social network. They are reserved and distant except with family members or intimate friends. They don't laugh as much as other kids do; their feelings always seem to be well under control. They're shy and silent, and they are lonely not because they are especially unlikable, but because they seem to have made a choice to remain apart or isolated. Does this mean they're depressed?

Not necessarily. What I've described here are aspects of temperament and personality, not symptoms of illness. Yet the distinction is difficult to make, and not all experts agree on what is a symptom of disease and what merely a normal variation in temperament. The problem is further complicated by the effect of personality on depression. Personality can predispose to depression, it can be a symptom of depression, it can modify the way a depression looks, and it can be altered by depression. The interaction between personality and depression is one of the most complicated problems in all of psychiatry.

We assume that traits of personality are more or less permanent, and that the symptoms of a disease will appear and disappear as the disease appears or disappears. Yet the fundamental view of psycho-analysis is that certain personality traits predispose people to depression, a position that seems intuitively correct: we all know people who seem by their nature less happy than others, and more prone to periods of deep pessimism or despair. Teenagers with dys-thymia, for example, will even describe themselves as "always like this—that's the way I am," but we know that they have an illness that can be treated. Or do we? How can we know really if what seem to be personality traits in these people are actually the symptoms of an illness and not an inherent part of the person's being? And it gets even more complicated: are there some people who tend toward depression but whose personalities are so unattractive or unsympa-thetic that they fail to gain the emotional support necessary to recovery? We know that we can't tell a depressed youngster to "snap out of it" and "stop acting so glum," but still, are some kids better equipped to survive a depressive episode because of their person-ality traits? These are questions not only of psychiatry and med-icine, but of philosophy, and they are far from being satisfactorily answered.

SADNESS WITHOUT DEPRESSION

Francesca, a lovely 17-year-old, grew up with a mother who had severe depressive episodes, repeatedly threatening suicide. Her ear-liest memories are of her mother leaving her by herself in the house while she took her older sister off to school. Her father left when she was ten or eleven, leaving her with the responsibility of taking care of her mother. She did well in school, had an active social life, but always kept herself somewhat removed. At times, she looked depressed, but she wasn't. She described herself as content, even if burdened in unusual ways. She viewed this as her fate, her bad luck. Everyone in her family agreed that it was her job to take care of her mother, and she did. Shortly after she left for college, her mother committed suicide.

Francesca was sad, no doubt about it, and with good reason. She had an unhappy life in many ways and a distrust about the future that was heartbreaking. Her college advisor suggested she talk to someone after her mother's death, so she came to see me. During our initial visit, it was clear that this girl had no symptoms that would respond to medication—she was depressed, in the loose sense of the term, but not in the psychiatric sense. Her life was far from perfect, and her mood matched her circumstances. Antidepressant medication does not make the world rosy. Francesca benefited from psychotherapy but did not need medication that would not have helped her.

It can be distressing for parents to see an adolescent who seems so different from the other kids, so isolated, lonely, or apparently unhappy, and they may seek psychiatric help to make their youngster be more like the other kids, "more normal." But psychiatrists are not good at altering personality traits, and insofar as a teenager is by her nature lonely or quiet or pessimistic, psychiatric treatment is unlikely to help. It may be more useful to find out if the youngster is content in her isolation, or if she would rather be different. If she herself wants change, then a therapist may be able to offer psychoanalytic, behavioral, or cognitive techniques that will be helpful. If she asks for psychiatric treatment, she should certainly get it—even if it's only to help determine that she doesn't really need treatment. But if she is comfortable in isolation, satisfied with her loneliness, accepting of her mood, there may be little a therapist can or should do about it. Some teens like this will find a comfortable place for themselves in adult life; those who do not can seek therapy then.

STRESSFUL LIFE EVENTS

We discussed stressful life events and their connection to depression in chapter 3, noting that these events can be depressing, but they don't in themselves cause depression. If you examine groups of adolescents who are depressed and compare them to groups who are not depressed, you don't find any difference in the number of stressful events they've undergone in the recent past. Thus it is a serious mistake to attribute a youngster's episode of depression to a specific recent unhappy event—that isn't what caused the illness, and the resolution of the unhappy event won't cure it.

But though this is true, it's only part of the story. If you look at the *kinds* of unhappy events the youngster has experienced, you get a very different picture. One study divided these unhappy events into "independent" and "dependent." The "independent" unhappy events were those over which the youngster had no control—a death in the family, a serious illness requiring hospitalization, foster care placement, divorce of the parents, and so on. The "dependent" unhappy events were those over which the youngster could be reasonably assumed to have some control—suspension from school, an unwanted pregnancy, breaking up with a boyfriend or girlfriend, an increase in the number of arguments with the parents, and others. Looking at the problems this way presented a marked contrast between depressed teenagers and healthy ones. The depressed teens had many more "dependent" unhappy events than the nondepressed.

IN THEIR OWN WORDS:
DIVORCE AND DEPRESSION

I was in tenth grade when my parents split up. That's when I really started to get depressed. After my dad left, my schoolwork started getting worse. I was sleeping a lot, and I was always in a bad mood. Nothing made me happy, not even baseball, which I love. I had a hard time concentrating. I really couldn't concentrate at all in school.

And then I felt bad physically, too. I'd wake up and I'd feel like I could go to sleep again for another whole day. Sometimes I'd stuff myself with food; other times I could skip meals without even feeling hungry.

People kept asking if I was OK, especially my mother. But I didn't feel like saying anything. I didn't feel like talking about it. Then finally I went to a psychiatrist. That helped a little, even though most of what I talked about was just the things that were happening to me right at that moment. My mom wanted me to go, so I went. I went for about a year. I really didn't talk to anyone else about it. My friends—I didn't know any of the kids very well in tenth grade—I never talked to my friends about it. I don't know if they noticed.

I never felt like killing myself; no, it never got that bad. My parents were really angry at each other, but then that calmed down a lot. I talked to the psychiatrist, but I think just time passing helped a lot. I never took any medicine. I thought a lot about what was going on, and I realized that it wasn't going to change, that it would never be like it was. I think I finally got used to that idea.

I think the worst part about being depressed was that I didn't enjoy anything. Nothing seemed like fun; nothing seemed interesting, no matter what I did. I knew something was wrong because I'm not a gloomy kid. But when my parents split up, everything got really bad. I just didn't feel like my normal self. Now I feel a lot better. I'm not always gloomy.

—Jeff, age 17

This same study produced another interesting result. The researchers found that depressed kids who experienced no dependent events were more severely depressed, more prone to anxiety, and had a more negative self-image than those who had experienced a dependent event. Their low self-esteem apparently made them subject to more severe depression, even in the absence of dependent unhappy events. It may be that low self-esteem lowers tolerance for stress—that is, kids with low self-esteem can be sent into a depression by much milder stresses than other kids.

Depression in teenagers is characterized by increased social and behavioral problems, problems that can persist even during remission or recovery from the episode of depression. We all experience stresses and unhappy events in life over which we have no control. But depressed kids experience unhappy events over which healthy kids *do* have some control. In other words, we can, loosely speaking, say that clinical depression leads to unhappy or stressful life events rather than the other way around. People will often say something like this: "No wonder she's depressed—look at the terrible things that have happened to her." It may be more accurate, at least in some cases, to say "No wonder terrible things have happened to her—she has an illness called depression."

DOES STRESS CAUSE DEPRESSION, OR DOES DEPRESSION CAUSE STRESS?

Justin's mother was a psychiatric social worker, his father a teacher. He was quite bright and doing fine in school, but by senior year, he'd begun to behave differently. He got involved with a wilder crowd and started seeing a girl who had an arrest record for drug use. The autumn after high school graduation, he started attending a college nearby, became more and more involved with the girl, and started using crack cocaine himself. Eventually, he lost his driver's license when he was convicted of driving while impaired. His parents forbade him from seeing the girl, but he defied them. He and his girlfriend began committing petty acts of vandalism, finally escalating to breaking into a house in the suburb in which they lived. He was arrested along with his girlfriend.

Justin was bright, good-looking, and intelligent, and he came from a stable and economically comfortable home—he had, in other words, everything a kid is supposed to have. But he was suffering from an untreated depression, and it is difficult to consider his problems without drawing some connection to his ailment. He was depressed, and you could say he was depressed because he was in so much trouble. But you could also just as truly say that at least one of the reasons he was in so much trouble was that he had, for at least several years, suffered from untreated depression.

LEARNING DISABILITIES

As recently as eight or ten years ago, not much was known about the emotional well-being of teenagers with learning disabilities. That's changing now, as researchers begin to examine this issue. They are learning that depression is very common among these youngsters. Studies have found rates of depression of up to 35 percent in groups of learning disabled teenagers. Among kids with learning disabilities, depression is clearly something to look for and treat.

My car mechanic likes to remind me that "you can have lice and fleas at the same time," meaning that a good mechanic doesn't stop looking for problems after he finds, say, a bad fuel pump—you can have a defective timing chain at the same time. Fixing only one of them won't get you to your destination. When I first interview a youngster, even after I decide that depression is the problem, my job isn't done. I look for other problems, both medical and psychiatric, and often I find them. If a therapist isn't looking for these other problems, she's only doing part of the job.

6

The Psychological Treatment of Depression

From the late nineteenth century until the middle of the twentieth, psychological theories of depression were at the forefront. Now that much more is known about the biological causes of and treatments for depression, this is no longer so. But this does not mean that the psychological dimension of depression is no longer of concern. On the contrary, it is clear that psychological and biological treatment of the illness are complementary—each works better when accompanied by the other.

Even if medicine is necessary, as it often is in cases of major depression, most adolescents do not see a psychiatrist first. They are more likely to see a school counselor, a social worker, or a psychologist, and well-trained people in these fields are able and qualified to provide helpful psychotherapy. In any case, the fact is that there aren't enough psychiatrists available who are willing to treat adolescents. I like teenagers myself, and find great satisfaction in treating them, but not all psychiatrists feel the same way. And anyway, a psychiatrist isn't necessary in every case.

Major depression is unquestionably a biological illness. But biological illnesses of all kinds—not just psychiatric illnesses—are affected by environmental and psychological stimuli. If a youngster is susceptible to the biological illness called depression, an unhappy event, a trip to an unfamiliar place, or a criticism from a teacher, parent, or friend are events that can trigger or worsen a depressive episode. In other words, the reason for the occurrence or severity of an episode of depression at a given moment can be psychological, and therefore psychological treatments are useful and appropriate in relieving symptoms.

I have one patient who perfectly illustrates the problem. Evelyn is a 17-year-old college student who initially came to me with severe anorexia. She had a three-year history of starving herself and purging by both laxative abuse and vomiting. During these years she had been in multiple treatments, including several hospitalizations when her weight became precariously low. She was referred again for inpatient treatment and evaluation for antidepressants, which in the past she had adamantly refused. Once I got her admitted I started her on Prozac to control the vomiting and also to address the depressive symptoms of irritability, decreased concentration, poor self-esteem, excessive tearfulness, and sleeplessness. The medication, along with the structured environment of the hospital with firm behavioral guidelines as to eating and weight loss, seemed to be having a positive effect. But in the course of the hospitalization I learned that she'd had an older brother who had died in a car accident when she was nine years old. She'd never mentioned this to anyone taking her history, and it was never a focus of therapy. When the information was uncovered in the course of a family meeting, Evelyn refused to discuss it, saying that she was over it and that it had nothing to do with her current problems. She also refused to attend any more family meetings, saying that she didn't want to involve her family in her problems. Although medication helped relieve her symptoms, it is clear that her brother's death will continue to prevent her recovery until she is able to understand its continuing effect on her. This is exactly the kind of problem that requires psychotherapy.

Psychological treatment also helps get a youngster to accept the diagnosis of depression and take the prescribed medication for it. Most youngsters (and most adults, too) are reluctant to accept the idea that they have a mental illness of any sort. The process of understanding and accepting this can be a long one for both the teenager and his parents, and family education to achieve both an intellectual understanding of the facts and a psychological acceptance of their consequences is essential. This is one of the reasons for books like this one.

For many reasons, psychological treatments are difficult to study scientifically—that is, it's hard to set up studies that result in scientifically accurate assessments of their effectiveness. The skills of the therapist and the quality of the therapy can vary; it's difficult to train all the therapists in a study to perform exactly the same kind of therapy; the match between a patient and a therapist can affect outcome sometimes as much as the kind of therapy used; some patients simply respond better to talk therapy than others. In other words, it's hard to know which factors are important and which not so in arriving at conclusions about effectiveness. All studies of psychotherapy must be considered with these limitations in mind.

There is some evidence that psychotherapy has physical effects on the brain, effects that can actually be measured, just as brain changes caused by drug therapy can be measured. These observed brain changes give biological support to what most therapists have believed all along: psychotherapy can be a powerfully beneficial treatment.

I find that I have to educate teenagers about therapy. It's important to set the parameters—what to expect, what may happen, how they may feel—and generally prepare them for what will go on. No one is born knowing how to benefit from therapy. Also, I try to get them curious about the process, about what they can learn about themselves. I compare it to a detective novel: we're looking for clues that can explain their feelings and their behaviors.

Therapy also enhances the ability to medicate effectively. If I have a relationship with a youngster, he is more likely to take the pills I prescribe, accept the treatment I've devised, than if I'm a distant figure he sees once every so often. An understanding of psychodynamics also informs what I will say to someone in treatment, how I'll phrase my interpretations, what interventions I will make, and so on. I focus here on a limited number of therapies that are among the most widely used and tested. Of course there are dozens, if not hundreds, of variations in psychotherapeutic methods, ranging from the perfectly conventional to the highly dubious, and practiced by a wide variety of people of various levels of training and expertise.

PSYCHOANALYTIC PSYCHOTHERAPY

Psychoanalytic therapy is derived from the theories of Sigmund Freud and other thinkers and is based on the premise that the exploration and understanding of unconscious emotional conflicts can improve functioning and relieve the symptoms of certain mental disorders. Through the 1950s most therapists believed that this was the best, if not the only, way to treat mental disorders, but the limitations of this approach have become more evident over time. Few believe that psychoanalytic psychotherapy is of much help in treating severe cases of major depression, and, although it can be helpful as an adjunctive therapy, almost no one would now recommend it as a first-line treatment. Psychoanalytic psychotherapy has two other distinct disadvantages as a treatment for depression: it usually takes a long time, and it is expensive. Still, classical psychoanalytic treatment has its place and can be quite helpful to depressed people under certain circumstances.

Sometimes briefer forms of psychological treatment (see below) don't work because the youngster can't be talked out of false ideas—irrational forces at work are too powerful. Sometimes youngsters who are psychologically minded are curious about what is driving these less rational feelings and are willing to undertake the self-exploration that is a part of psychoanalytic psychotherapy.

Problems often remain even after depression is treated—social problems, milder forms of unhappiness, unresolved grief over loss by death or divorce, and so on. Insofar as personality factors increase the risk of depression, psychoanalytic psychotherapy may be of some help. In addition, this form of treatment offers an intense relationship with the therapist, which can in itself be meaningful and helpful. Adolescence is a time of confusion, and open-ended discussion with an objective listener may help a vulnerable youngster sort out some problems.

In psychoanalysis, the analyst traditionally remains a neutral and noncritical figure. In the treatment of adolescents, I've found that this is not always possible. I have to be actively on their side, and if they are doing something dangerous I want to be able to stop them. Being detached and strictly analytic in such situations does not work. Classical analytic techniques where the analyst encourages self-exploration but remains somewhat neutral and interprets the transference—that is, the duplication in the therapeutic situation of feelings and relationships that the adolescent may have with others in his life—are difficult to use with many adolescents. Adolescents require real relationships and they expect reactions, generally supportive, from therapists. Therapists also need the ability to engage patients in treatment. In the case of adolescents, a neutral or remote stance on the part of the therapist may not provide enough of an opportunity for an emotional connection. Psychoanalytic techniques probably work best when there is a degree of curiosity and willingness on the part of the adolescent to take a hard look at patterns of behavior and internal conflicts. This is a tall order even for most adults—it's the unusual teenager who can handle it.

INTERPERSONAL PSYCHOTHERAPY

In the late 1930s, a group of psychoanalysts led by Harry Stack Sullivan, Erich Fromm, Karen Horney, and others began to believe that classical Freudian psychoanalysis underestimated the influence of social and cultural phenomena in explaining human behavior, both normal and abnormal. While Freudians believed that emotional conflicts developed from instinctual drives, these therapists felt that they arose from relationships with others, both real and imagined. Thus was born interpersonal psychotherapy, or IPT.

As its name suggests, IPT concentrates on improving the relationships of the patient with the significant people in his life. This involves improving the patient's communications skills and concentrating on the specific problems the patient is facing right now. At the outset, the therapist explains to a depressed patient that his disorder is a medical illness with unpleasant physical and psychological symptoms, but an illness that can be treated by, among other things, this form of psychotherapy. Treatment is usually brief, but it can also go on for extended periods of time. The therapist concentrates on several areas: dealing with grief, successfully undergoing life transitions (moving to a new school or starting a new relationship), finding methods of resolving disputes and disagreements, and communicating successfully with friends, family, or schoolmates. Failures in any of these areas can lead to depression, and the aim is to identify the specific areas involved and to relieve and prevent depression by finding behavioral strategies that work. Unlike cognitive therapy, which concentrates on rational or intellectual approaches to behavior, or psychoanalytic therapy, which explores unconscious motivations, IPT focuses on figuring out how a given approach to interactions with others makes the patient feel and discovering approaches that make her feel better.

IPT makes no assertion about the origins of depression, but holds that the symptoms can be relieved by solving interpersonal problems. The therapist will, in cooperation with the teenager, select a problem area from one of several—grief, role dispute, role transition, or interpersonal deficits—to serve as the focus of the therapy. Conflict with a boyfriend, trouble with teachers, the loss of a loved one, or an important transition in life like going to college may serve as the central issue or issues. The therapy does not dwell on the past, but concentrates on problems the patient is facing in the here and now. The treatment usually consists of about sixteen weekly sessions, but can go on longer.

IPT has been widely tested in treating major depression, and the largest study was carried out among more than two hundred patients at three different sites in the 1980s. Groups of patients were assigned to one of four treatment regimes: IPT, cognitive-behavioral therapy, imipramine (an antidepressant; see chapter 8), or placebo. All four groups showed improvement, but there were significant differences in the amount of improvement produced. Imipramine was a little better than IPT, and IPT was considerably better than cognitive-behavioral therapy. The three treatments were significantly better than placebo. Both imipramine and IPT were found to be better for more severe cases of depression. IPT has also been found effective in preventing relapse; in fact it is almost as effective as imipramine.

COGNITIVE-BEHAVIORAL THERAPY

Various kinds of behavioral therapies share certain theoretical characteristics. In all of them, the patient learns about the nature of his difficulties and the reasons for pursuing this particular kind of therapy to find relief. The therapies usually include homework and exercises that the patient practices outside of the therapy. They are highly structured, unlike insight therapies. Among the behavioral therapies, cognitive therapy is perhaps the most widely used, and almost certainly the most widely tested.

Cognitive-behavioral therapy has been studied extensively in the treatment of depression, and although it has certain limitations, it can be an effective treatment in many cases. Cognitive theory holds that people become depressed because they think in maladaptive ways—that is, errors in their thinking cause their depression. This is based on the assumption that environmental stimuli trigger thoughts, that the thoughts are then given personal meaning, and that this act causes various kinds of physical and psychological responses in the individual. Of particular concern are negative "automatic thoughts." These are thoughts that occur in rapid succession, stimulating painful emotional reactions and leading to helplessness and withdrawal. Whatever problems the person is facing while these automatic thoughts occur become more difficult to solve, leading to feelings of depression. The depression, in turn, causes maladaptive behavior, which then generates more negative thoughts and feelings, creating a vicious circle. Although we all have these automatic thoughts, they are more frequent in those who suffer from depression.

The theory lays out various kinds of cognitive errors that people make. For example, some engage in emotional reasoning: "I feel this way, therefore I am this way." Sometimes overgeneralization is the problem: "I didn't do well on this test, so it's obvious that I'll never do well on a test like this." Some people misinterpret ordinary physiological events (an increased heart rate, dizziness) as definitive indications of impending catastrophe or death. Others label themselves incorrectly: "I failed to get into that Ivy League college, so I am a failure." Some youngsters personalize events, interpreting any setback, however minor, as proof positive that they are bad people. All of this, according to cognitive theory, causes depression, and the depression can be relieved once the teenager understands the errors he is making.

Many studies show that depressed people experience these kinds of disturbances in the ways they process information, and that they are so common they can be considered one of the features of depression. In cognitive therapy, patients are taught to recognize these kinds of faulty logic in their automatic thoughts, and to develop alternatives that are more accurate and more helpful.

In addition, cognitive therapy examines the patient's underlying "schema," or core beliefs. These are the basic rules a person uses to interpret information he receives from the environment, and the rules can be either adaptive or maladaptive. Changing these core beliefs is more difficult than learning to deal with automatic thoughts, but it is important in reducing the risk of relapse.

Cognitive therapy is short term, usually lasting between ten and twenty sessions. A number of behavioral techniques are used, including activity scheduling and graded task assignments. Better cognition is thought to lead to better behavior, and better behavior to better understanding. The therapist actively collaborates with the patient, focusing on practical solutions to current problems, using examples from the patient's life to illustrate how inaccurate thoughts lead to maladaptive behavior and how cognition and behavior can both be changed for the better. The patient is encouraged to keep written records of dysfunctional thoughts, taught to recognize cognitive errors by examining the evidence, and shown how to develop alternate methods of thinking. The latter stages of the therapy concentrate on developing methods of dealing with stress, techniques that will prevent relapse after therapy is concluded.

Cognitive therapy in the treatment of depression generally works better in milder cases than in severe cases, although it can be used along with medication in severe cases. In some severe cases that are initially treated with antidepressant medication, cognitive therapy is about as effective as continued drug treatment in preventing relapse. Although there is considerable disagreement among professionals about the value of cognitive therapy compared to taking psychiatric medication, there is wide agreement that combining cognitive therapy with drug therapy is more effective than either approach alone.

To sum up, studies have produced varying results, but there is now general agreement that cognitive therapy is an effective treatment for mild depression, and it is also effective in preventing relapse in severe depressions that have been treated with psychotropic drugs. It is not, however, effective as a first-line treatment for severe depression.

COGNITIVE TECHNIQUES WITH TEENAGERS

Some teenagers do well when treated with both medicine and cognitive techniques. The combination often works well with youngsters who are not psychologically minded, or are disinclined to talk in the way psychoanalytically oriented psychotherapy requires.

Sally was a senior in high school, who had been accepted and was ready to go off to a good college. She became withdrawn, stopped seeing her friends, stopped eating, had crying fits for no apparent reason. The immediate cause was a breakup with her boyfriend who had "dumped" her for someone else. However, upon further exploration, it became clear that she had suffered major trauma during her childhood. This included physical abuse when she was two or three at the hands of her biological father, who had been diagnosed with paranoid schizophrenia. Her mother, whom she adored, had remarried and she had been raised by her stepfather, with whom she had a very conflicted relationship, at times openly hostile.

Sally had a bad history: one parent lost custody of her because of abuse, the other remarried. There was psychiatric illness in her family. It was clear that part of the reason she was depressed was that going away to college was reviving the unhappy feelings of her childhood experiences with separation. But she didn't understand this and didn't want to talk about it. However, she was willing and able to talk about how to avoid situations in which she would see her boyfriend, and how to redirect her energies so she could eliminate the problem from her mind.

We worked out, along cognitive lines, solutions to specific concrete problems. Sally was not a kid who wanted to talk about her childhood trauma—she wanted solutions to current problems, so that's what we concentrated on. The antidepressant medicine she was taking helped with crying spells and eating problems, which are difficult to control with cognitive techniques. The cognitive techniques, however, provided her with practical help to make her daily life more pleasant and her mood happier. This happens with many teenagers, in varying degrees. You have to use what works, whether it's psychodynamic, behavioral, cognitive, or pharmacological.

FAMILY THERAPY

Among the psychological factors in depression that have been studied is the role of other family members. Although it is clear that parents do not cause depression in youngsters, depression has nevertheless been shown to be associated with various kinds of family problems or difficult family relationships. For example, high levels of distress in the mother, poor quality of the parents' marriage, and a poor relationship between an adolescent and a father have all been shown to be associated with higher levels of depression in teenagers. Of course, it is important to remember that depression itself causes difficult relationships between people, so it is not easy to separate cause from effect in such situations.

Expressed emotion (EE) is a concept that describes the quality of a patient's relationship with his or her family. EE measures the extent to which a patient's family expresses criticism of the patient or is overinvolved in her life. A negative statement about the patient, evidence of overprotectiveness, even excessive praise of the patient is considered an indication of high expressed emotion in the patient's family. Such measures have been used to estimate rates of relapse in schizophrenia as well as depression. The theory holds that in families with high expressed emotion, relapse in depression is more likely.

This is a highly controversial theory. Some view this as "blaming the family" for the disease, a position now largely rejected by most experts. Others feel the studies purporting to show that EE has something to do with depression or its relapse are flawed, inadequately designed, or poorly carried out. Deciding whether a family is "overinvolved with" or "highly critical of" or "excessively prais-ing" a patient is largely a subjective judgment on the part of an interviewer, no matter how elaborate and sophisticated the statisti-cal evaluation of the resulting data may be. Most of the studies that have been done about the effect of criticism by a family of a patient show, at most, a weak association between criticism and relapse.

One recent study found little evidence that adolescents with major depression were from families any more "dysfunctional" than those of nondepressed adolescents. The researchers found that 44 percent of the families with depressed adolescents were in the healthy range and almost one-third of families without depressed youngsters were in the dysfunctional range.

I try to leave discussions of ideology aside and get the parents involved in the treatment in ways that might help their adolescent cope with a crisis. I spend a lot of time educating families about depression, what might cause it, what works in helping communi-cation, and so on. Many parents have tremendous difficulty with the idea that their child is depressed. They may feel tremendously guilty, particularly if they have been depressed or have other family members who are depressed. Some parents, however, deny the extent of a child's illness and minimize what the child is experienc-ing: "How can she be depressed? She has everything. She's just looking for attention." These parents may see the child's symptoms as a manipulation or hostility directed at them.

INTERVENING WITH THE FAMILY

Pamela was the only child of two highly intelligent older parents. She proved quite gifted from an early age and delighted her parents with her talents in language and mathematics. When she was 4, a serious heart condition was discovered. After undergoing surgery, Pamela developed a metabolic condition that required around the clock medication. Her parents were in charge of this, and their con-scientiousness undoubtedly saved her life. However, her condition also created an emotional overinvolvement as well as a physical dependence, especially because she required this treatment for several years. As time went by, her separation anxiety increased to the point that when she entered high school she became quite depressed, losing interest in school and activities. She was fearful of growing up and having to leave her parents, and at the same time very angry at her continuing need for them. She had grown so dependent on them that whenever she needed anything she called her parents to help.

For Pamela, treatment, which continued through much of high school, involved individual insight-oriented therapy, antidepres-sants, and ongoing family interventions to enable everyone to sep-arate in a positive way.

I tell this story not to imply that most families act in destructive ways, nor to blame families for anything, but to say that there are occasions when intervention with the family can be highly useful. Child rearing is an imperfect art. Pamela needed an unusual level of care for illness, and there probably was no perfect way to handle the worry and anxiety that comes with having a medically ill child. There is no such thing as perfect parenting or perfect parenting technique.

Certainly enlisting the aid of the family in helping an ill young-ster is important. The family is an essential ally in helping the teen-ager overcome her illness. But blaming the family for the illness is just plain wrong. So though there are clear benefits in having a sym-pathetic family to help in making a treatment successful, it is impor-tant to remember that the depression is a disease of an individual teenager, and it is the individual teenager who must be treated.

What Is the Role of the Family?

Although families don't cause depression, they can play a very important role in its treatment. The family needs a united approach. A depressed youngster needs support—not excuses, but understanding. The family can't use the illness against the kid, and the kid can't be allowed to use the illness as an excuse. At the very least, the family has to be neutral—parents and others in the family may not be able to make it better, but it is always possible to make it worse.

I try to get the family in to discuss it. "What can we do here to make it easier for everyone in the family to deal with the illness of one of its members?" I'll ask. "Can you tell me what the circumstances are when you have a fight, when you yell at her and she yells back? Give me an example of what happens. Is there a way to avoid these situations?" If the family starts to feel they are the adversary of the therapist, that's not helpful. Therefore I work to form an alliance with the family, trying to make them aware that they have a role in the treatment, even though it's the teenager who is suffering from the disease.

Families can't be allowed to be hopeless, and there isn't any reason for them to feel that way. Most kids get better, and the fact that families are willing to bring them in and give them support is the most hopeful sign. Here a psychoanalytic perspective can be quite helpful. Families can be reassured that time is on the side of teenagers—they're going to grow up, moving through developmental stages, and they're going to get better. The family is not the child's therapist, but they do have to represent a hopeful point of view. I try to point out when I think they're doing the wrong thing—having false expectations, minimizing the problem or feeling overwhelmed by it, or feeling guilty about the effect on the other kids in the family. Depression is hard on everyone, but the family has to remember that it's hardest of all on the person who has it.

CHOOSING A THERAPEUTIC APPROACH

Most good psychotherapists draw from all of these theoretical posi-
tions, choosing what works best and creating a therapeutic approach
designed for an individual patient. Where behavioral techniques
work, I use them; where exploring unconscious motivation is helpful, I use psychoanalytic techniques; if there are family problems, I
get the family involved, and so on. The first-line treatment for
severe major depression is drug therapy—any doctor who recommends anything else as the primary treatment is offering substan-
dard care. But it is clear that in preventing relapse and providing
continuing care, psychotherapy—in the hands of a competent practitioner, no matter what the theoretical approach—can be useful.
Some believe it is almost as useful as continuing drug therapy. It is
also clear that drug treatment in combination with psychotherapy is
a better treatment than either drugs or psychotherapy alone.

I've tried to outline in this chapter what is known scientifically
about some of the kinds of psychotherapy used to treat depression.
But much remains unknown, of course, and a therapist in the real
world needs to make choices about how to proceed with individual
patients who may or may not respond the way the studies say they
should. This is why I use a combination of treatments, or move to
another treatment when one doesn't work, or design a combination
of psychological and psychopharmacological treatments specifically for an individual patient. This is where the experience, skills,
and clinical judgment of a therapist come into play in treating real
patients with serious illness.

7

What Kind of Care?: The Health Professionals Who Treat Depression, What They Do, and Where They Work

Because there are many kinds of mental health care professionals, knowing who does what is important in finding the best care. In most states, anyone, even someone with no training at all, can call himself a "psychotherapist" and practice "psychotherapy." It is easy to imagine that not all such practitioners will be helpful to someone with a mental disorder. Some can be quite dangerous. It's important to know what the various specialties do, and what they can do for a teenager with depression.

Most state governments have an office that oversees the licensing of professionals and can provide information on whether the professional in question has ever been disciplined. Directories of professionals can also provide information about academic background and field of specialty. It is best to avoid professionals who do not have professional degrees and have had limited training in working with patients. Academic medical centers are a good place to go for references for all health professionals, including mental health providers.

Many people immediately go to the Internet for information about medical professionals, but searching with a computer may be no more reliable than looking in the telephone book—which is to say that it may not be reliable at all. Anyone who wants to can list his or her name and address on a Web site, without any authorization from the state government or any professional organization. There are dozens, if not hundreds, of sites that list therapists of all sorts with assertions about mental health and claims of proficiency in treating mental illness that range from reasonable to outlandish. The Internet is filled with information, true and false, and each Web site should be treated with some degree of skepticism.

MENTAL HEALTH CARE PROFESSIONALS

Psychiatrists

Psychiatrists are medical doctors who have either an M.D. degree or a D.O. degree (doctor of osteopathy). They are licensed by the state in which they practice. Like all doctors, they have graduated from college and spent four years in medical school. Psychiatry, like other medical specialties, usually requires four further years of training: a year of medical internship plus three years of psychiatric residency. (Further specialized training in child or adolescent psychiatry can add another two years.) This training is intense: it includes work in neurology, emergency care, child and adolescent psychiatry, and general medical care, and involves seeing hundreds of patients with the full range of psychiatric disorders. The training is—take it from me—exhaustive and exhausting.

After the training is completed, psychiatrists usually take an examination administered by the American Board of Psychiatry and Neurology that includes a written exam and an oral exam in which the psychiatrist-in-training examines patients and then is orally quizzed by two examiners about the patients' diagnosis and treatment. A psychiatrist doesn't have to be "board certified" to practice psychiatry, and there are certainly competent psychiatrists who have not taken this examination, but being board certified implies a basic competence that is surely desirable. If you're looking for a psychiatrist, picking one who is board certified is a good idea. Some psychiatrists specialize in geriatric treatment, children and adolescents, substance abuse treatment, or psychoanalysis. Some of these specialties require extra training; some do not. Usually, the extra training is referred to as a "fellowship," except for psychoanalysis, where a trainee is usually called a "candidate." There are board certifications in geriatrics and substance abuse, child and adolescent psychiatry, forensic psychiatry, and addiction psychiatry, but at this time there is no board certification in psychopharmacology.

Psychiatrists, because they are trained in medicine, can evaluate the extent to which physical illness plays a role in psychiatric disorders. Moreover, treating major depression almost always involves prescribing medicine, and psychiatrists, the only medical doctors among the mental health professionals, are the ones usually responsible for doing this. (Nurse practitioners and physicians' assistants can, under the supervision of an M.D., prescribe medicine.) Of course, other doctors can prescribe psychiatric medicines, too; in fact most antidepressants are prescribed by general practitioners. Unfortunately, general practitioners, with all the good will in the world, often err in prescribing these medicines, giving the wrong doses, failing to stick with a treatment long enough, failing to try different drugs or different regimens when the first thing they try doesn't work or causes unpleasant side effects. Studies have shown that people recover from depression faster when they are treated by a psychiatrist. In general, the more serious the disorder, the more likely a psychiatrist will be the most important member of the treatment team.

Some psychiatrists specialize in psychopharmacology—the use of medicines to treat disorders. Often an assessment by a psychopharmacologist is useful if a youngster is not responding to the usual pharmacological treatments. Sometimes, a treating psychiatrist will recommend a consultation with such a specialist when ordinary drug regimens don't seem to work.

Although many psychiatrists (like me) treat both adults and teenagers, some specialize in treating adolescents and children. A psychiatrist who specializes in child and teenager psychiatry has had the same training as any psychiatrist (four years of medical school, a year of medical internship, and two or three years of psychiatric residency). In addition, he or she has had one or more years of supervised training working with children, adolescents, and their families. After completing all this training, the psychiatrist is eligible to take the examination to become board certified in psychiatry, and, with an additional exam, board certified in child and adolescent psychiatry.

If you consult a board-certified psychiatrist, you know that you are seeing someone with medical training who has spent a minimum of three years diagnosing and treating people with mental illness. This experience alone, even before considering any other qualifications, gives some confidence in the practitioner's expertise. Psychiatrists, it must be said, also charge more for their services than other mental health professionals.

Psychologists

The American Psychological Association, the largest professional association of psychologists, offers this definition of psychology: "Psychology is the study of the mind and behavior. The discipline embraces all aspects of the human experience—from the functions of the brain to the actions of nations, from child development to care for the aged. In every conceivable setting from scientific research centers to mental health care services, 'the understanding of behavior' is the enterprise of psychologists."

A psychologist usually holds a Ph.D. or a Psy.D. (Doctor of Psychology) degree, though some have master's degrees only. Psychologists may be "experimental psychologists" or "clinical psychologists." Clinical psychologists practice psychotherapy with patients. Experimental psychologists work in theoretical areas of human and animal behavior and do not usually see patients for psychotherapy.

A doctorate in psychology usually entails at least five years of course work in psychological theory, statistics, and various psychotherapeutic techniques, plus some supervised clinical work.

Some psychologists specialize in administering and interpreting psychological tests; some practice psychotherapy using various techniques and theoretical perspectives. Some psychologists take a competency examination administered by the American Board of Professional Psychology, and in all fifty states clinical psychologists must pass licensing examinations.

Psychologists trained in psychotherapeutic techniques often provide the psychotherapy part of the treatment of depression. They have been instrumental in developing the cognitive-behavioral techniques for treating depression (discussed in chapter 6). It is common for a youngster to see a psychologist for talk therapy and, if necessary, have the psychologist consult with a psychiatrist for the pharmacological part of the treatment.

Psychologists also administer psychological testing to help diagnose and measure the progress of treatment in psychiatric illnesses. Psychologists cannot prescribe medicine, however, and to the extent that depression is a physical illness with behavioral manifestations, its treatment may involve medical understanding of the human body. Therefore, if medication becomes necessary, a referral would normally be made to a psychiatrist who understands the complex interactions of various drugs with each other, their side effects, and their effect on the functioning of the human body. Any experienced psychologist will be able to recognize the need for medication, understand its effects, and work closely with a psychiatrist in identifying proper regimens and seeing to it that the youngster follows them.

Psychiatrists and Other Professionals Working Together

I am the medical director for an eating disorders program with a professional staff that consists of Ph.D.-level psychologists and social workers. My job is to evaluate any new patients for the presence of underlying depression, anxiety, or other psychiatric illness that may be influencing the patient's progress. A percentage of the people I see require medication. I then prescribe medication and follow up monthly with input from the psychologists and social workers. I rely on the clinical judgment of the professionals who work day to day with these patients. I feel comfortable in doing this because I know that these people are competent to call in psychiatric help when they need it.

Ordinarily, the process is routine. Eating disorders rarely require emergency care. But every once in a while, I need to intervene. One girl was very preoccupied with weight, eating, and food, and they were treating her as an anorexic. But in the course of my evaluation, I found she had a psychotic disorder, and the eating problems were merely a symptom of this much more serious disease. On another occasion, I met the patient at the clinic's headquarters and actually walked her across the street to the hospital because she was suicidal and needed immediate hospitalization.

Often, psychologists work with one or two psychiatrists for medication evaluations. Suppose a teenager is in psychotherapy with a psychologist, but over the course of time it becomes clear that the symptoms are not responding to talk therapy alone. At that point, the psychologist may recommend that the child get an evaluation for medication from a psychiatrist. This can occur through referral to a private psychiatrist, to one available through the teenager's covering health plan, or to a local mental health clinic. Cost considerations often play a part in deciding which option to pursue.

Understand that this can be a time-consuming process. Often the first person you call will not have time to see the youngster. Referral lists from your health insurance provider often include psychiatrists who have left the area, retired, or who do not treat adolescents. Not every psychiatrist wants to do medication management, especially if they don't know the therapist. Some simply don't have time to see any new patients. But even when you've passed these barriers, the job isn't done. You will have to try to establish the suitability of this doctor for your teenager's problem. You need to feel like you have an ally in the process, so even phone impressions are important. When you meet, you have to ask yourself and the doctor some questions: Are you comfortable with this doctor? Has this doctor had experience with psychopharmacology, and specifically with the psychopharmacological treatment of adolescents? How long has he or she been in practice? What will the plan be? How often will it be necessary to see the child? How involved will this doctor be in the treatment? There are no right or wrong answers to these questions, but you need information about how the treatment is going to go forward.

If you can't find a psychiatrist on your health insurance provider's list, or aren't satisfied with the ones you've found, you can go back to the insurer with the recommendation of your child's therapist and ask the insurance company to negotiate a price with this recommended therapist. This is particularly important to do if you can't find someone in your area or can't locate someone who specializes in adolescent psychiatry or psychopharmacology.

Sometimes it may be worth it to pay the price for private care. If an adolescent has a good relationship with her psychotherapist, she will want to follow his advice and see the person he recommends. The number of visits may be limited, which will keep down the cost. In the end this may be the best solution, even if it isn't the cheapest.

Social Workers

A professional social worker has a degree in social work and meets state legal requirements for licensure. Professional social workers practice in many settings, including family service agencies, child welfare agencies, community mental health centers, private practice, schools, hospitals, and employee assistance programs, among others. Those with experience in treating people with psychiatric problems are often called "clinical social workers" or "psychiatric social workers." Like psychologists, they often work in collaboration with psychiatrists. Professional social workers are the nation's largest group of mental health service providers.

Social workers who work with patients usually have a master's degree, which may be an M.S.W. (Master of Social Work) or an

M.S. (Master of Science), depending on the degree issued by the school they attended. Some have a D.S.W. (Doctor of Social Work) degree (the extra degree may be evidence of training for research or teaching rather than psychotherapy). A master's degree in social work usually requires two years of classroom instruction, plus supervised clinical practice.

Social workers with ACSW (Association of Certified Social Workers) after their names have been accredited by the National Association of Social Workers. They have at least two years of postgraduate experience as a social worker, and have completed a written examination administered by the National Association of Social Workers. Social workers are licensed or certified in all fifty states, but the requirements for licensure or certification vary widely from one state to another.

In practice, social workers are on the front lines in treating adolescents. They are often the first person a youngster sees in treatment, and many times seeing a social worker will be sufficient treatment for a teenager in difficulty.

Psychiatric Nurses and Nurse Practitioners

Psychiatric nurse specialists have a master's degree in nursing and are certified by the American Nursing Association. Psychiatric nurse practitioners have a period of supervised practice followed by at least two years of independent practice and have passed a qualifying national examination. Psychiatric nurse practitioners have additional specialty training in psychiatry and in many states are permitted to prescribe medicine. They may work in hospitals, clinics, or in private practice independently of psychiatrists or other medical doctors. (There are nurse practitioners in many other specialties as well.)

Someone called a "psychiatric nurse" may simply be a nurse with no more special training than any other nurse, but who works with psychiatric patients. They can be certified by the American Nursing Association as "psychiatric mental health nurses."

In hospitals, psychiatric nurses are responsible for the day-to-day operations of the setting in which patients live. They document patients' behavior, and they share their observations with psychiatrists and other members of the hospital staff.

Pastoral Counselors

Pastoral counselors are clergy and others who counsel people with psychological problems or problems in living. Their training varies widely, from people who have doctorates in theology and psychology and years of supervised training in psychotherapy, to those who have barely any training at all. A certifying organization called the American Association of Pastoral Counselors requires its members to complete three years of study at a seminary as well as a master's or doctoral program that includes training in crisis intervention. But no license is required to perform pastoral counseling, and many pastoral counselors are simply members of the clergy who offer a combination of psychological and spiritual advice to their parishioners. Such therapists, depending on their experience and training, may be helpful to some people.

Any clergy member with a counseling degree is trained to know when the skills of another mental health professional are required.

Occupational Therapists

Occupational therapists aid patients, both medical and psychiatric, in increasing independent functioning and overcoming disability. The term "occupational" doesn't necessarily refer to employment, but to any meaningful activity in a person's life. For a patient with a psychiatric illness, the occupational therapist will focus on helping in managing time, working productively with others, and enjoying leisure activities.

An accredited occupational therapist has completed an educational program accredited by the American Occupational Therapy

Association's certifying arm, the Accreditation Council for Occupational Therapy. This involves at least a bachelor's degree and often a master's degree. All OT education programs include a period of supervised clinical experience.

Occupational therapists who specialize in mental health usually work as staff members in psychiatric hospitals, although there are private practitioners as well.

Recreational Therapists

Recreational therapists provide rehabilitation services to restore independence through recreational activities. In physical rehabilitation, a recreational therapist might use a recreational activity, such as fishing, to help a patient with right-side paralysis resume his leisure activity by using his left side. In a psychiatric setting the recreational therapist may help a depressed patient gain greater self-confidence and independence and increase the quality of the person's life through leisure activities. Recreational therapists work in hospitals, both psychiatric and medical, as members of an interdisciplinary team.

Recreational therapists are certified by the National Council for Therapeutic Recreation Certification. A few states regulate this profession through licensure or certification, but most do not.

Other Therapists

Certified clinical mental health counselors are a relatively new specialty among mental health professionals, developed over the past twenty years. These practitioners hold a master's degree, granted after two years of study in counseling that includes clinical as well as classroom work. They are certified by the National Board for Certified Counselors, which administers an examination (the National Counselor Examination for Licensure and Certification) and issues credentials that are recognized in most states, but not all. A certified clinical mental health counselor has at least 3,000 hours of postgraduate supervised practice and has passed the examination. The NBCC offers specialty certification in several areas in addition to clinical mental health counseling, including career counseling, school counseling, and addiction counseling.

Any of the therapists mentioned above may do *family and marriage counseling*, and in some states, although not all, such therapists are licensed. It is not unusual for a therapist to meet with the family concerning a youngster's progress, but this is not the same as family therapy. A psychiatrist may refer a family for therapy, or refer a couple for couples therapy, but he or she would normally do so only in the context of the adolescent's treatment. A youngster who is depressed and also has an eating disorder, for example, might require family treatment as well.

Psychoanalysts are neither psychiatrists nor psychologists but have trained in the techniques of psychoanalysis at institutes that specialize in such training. *Certified addiction counselors*, recognized by certain professional organizations and, to varying extents, by some state governments, may help a depressed youngster who is also abusing substances.

These many different kinds of mental health professionals work in various settings, from private practice offices to large academic medical centers, and depressed teenagers are often helped considerably by working with them. In serious cases of clinical depression—and most mental health professionals know a serious case when they see one—the professional most suited to treating an adolescent will almost certainly be a psychiatrist. Still, most teenagers will likely see another mental health professional first, and only arrive in a psychiatrist's office if their symptoms do not remit.

A profession that is licensed (as opposed to being certified by a professional organization or association) meets standards set by the state government, and licenses are subject to discipline by a state board. In general, this means that licensing requires stricter standards of training and practice. In all states, psychiatrists, psychologists, nurses, and social workers are licensed. Insurers are generally more willing to cover care by licensed professionals, though on the other hand insurers are also interested in minimizing the amount of care they pay for. Since licensed professionals generally have higher fees than unlicensed practitioners, this may create a conflict between the insurer and the parent or teenager trying to seek the best possible care.

MENTAL HEALTH CARE FACILITIES

Most youngsters will see a psychiatrist or other professional in a private office, but hospitalization may be required for teenagers who are more seriously ill, especially if they are suicidal. Just as individual practitioners are licensed and monitored in various ways, so are health care facilities. What follows is a description of the kinds of mental health treatment facilities now available.

Major Medical Centers

These are large hospital complexes, generally located in urban areas and often affiliated with a medical school. A separate psychiatry department within the center offers a broad range of traditional psychiatric treatments, and usually also administers a psychiatric research component.

The research components of these institutions, since they offer treatments that are new or still being studied, are particularly useful for teenagers who do not respond to the usual treatments. If a patient's case is suitable for one of these studies, treatment, including hospitalization, is usually offered without charge. Most of what we know about effective psychiatric treatment grows out of such research programs.

In order to qualify to do research, institutions have to meet strict standards, and no adolescent would be allowed to participate in research that is potentially harmful. If a teenager is going to participate in a study, she and her parents will have the entire process carefully explained to them, and they will have to sign a consent form outlining exactly how the study will be carried out and how the youngster will participate in it. No teenager can be involved in a research project without the full understanding and consent of the adolescent and his or her parents.

The type of follow-up care to be provided will also be specified in the consent form. Consent forms are sometimes written in highly technical language, so it is important to have conversations with research staff about the project and how it will be carried out. Studies have shown that many participants in research projects either do not read or do not understand the consent forms. Don't be one of them. Teenager and parents alike must read the consent form carefully, and ask for explanations of anything they do not understand. Only after they are satisfied with the answers should they sign the form. Remember also that signing the form does not mean you have to continue with the research program if you don't want to—you can drop out of it any time you like.

Research is overseen by an institutional review board, or IRB. Any institution that does research is required to have an IRB, which consists of both researcher and nonresearcher members. The IRB carefully reviews every study, often using guidelines set by the federal government.

Although psychiatric research is sometimes portrayed as cavalier or insensitive, the characterization is not accurate. The protocols that an adolescent might be suitable for would involve responses to medications that have already been tested in adults, or responses to nonmedical interventions in combination with medicine. The most invasive procedure in such studies would be a blood test, and noninvasive procedures might include CAT scans or MRIs. All of the details of what is to happen during a study are made clear before a youngster enters such a program.

Large medical centers are a good source of referrals for all medical and psychiatric problems.

Private Psychiatric Hospitals

Although there is a great deal of variation among private psychiatric hospitals, they are in general small (ranging from about 40 to 150 beds) and have staff-to-patient ratios that are better than public hospitals or medical center facilities. Some specialize in alcohol and substance abuse rehabilitation, eating disorders, or adolescents; others are general psychiatric hospitals which offer a range of treatments to different kinds of patients. The Joint Commission on Accreditation of Hospitals examines hospitals to ascertain whether they meet a basic standard of care, and it is worth checking to be sure that the hospital is accredited by this organization. Your youngster will very likely be directed to a particular private psychiatric hospital that has a contract with your insurer.

Community Hospitals

These are smaller hospitals, usually not affiliated with a medical center or medical school. The psychiatric staff may be quite small—sometimes there is no separate psychiatric facility, and psychiatric patients are housed along with other patients. Some community hospitals do not have full-time psychiatrists on their staffs at all and rely on outside doctors under contract. The quality of treatment can vary considerably from one hospital to another, and may not be the best solution for a teenager who needs to be hospitalized.

Public Hospitals

Public hospitals are run by the state or municipalities, and every state has them. They offer mental health care to patients who could otherwise not afford it. They offer a range of psychiatric services, including long-term care for severely mentally ill patients. Although some of these facilities provide good care, many are negatively affected by poor funding, offering staff-to-patient ratios that are not as good as at other hospitals. The first hospitalization for an adolescent would rarely be in this kind of public institution, which is largely devoted to patients with chronic psychiatric disorders.

Freestanding Clinics

These small facilities offer outpatient mental health care, usually subsidized by government grants, and often base their fees on ability to pay. They may be run by a group of psychiatrists or function as a subsidiary of a hospital or medical center. In addition to individual treatment, these facilities often offer group therapy both for patients and their families. If the clinic is attached to a hospital that is accredited by the Joint Commission on the Accreditation of Health Care Organizations (JCAHO), then it must meet the JCAHO's standards for ambulatory care. You can ask whether the clinic is inspected, and if so by whom. In New York State, for example, facilities that collect Medicare or Medicaid payments must be certified by the state, which means that almost all outpatient programs are so certified.

Psychiatric Emergency Rooms

There is considerable variation in the quality of psychiatric care offered in hospital emergency rooms. In medical centers in large cities, where emergency rooms are staffed by psychiatric residents and attending psychiatrists, the care can be excellent. In smaller hospitals and in rural areas, it may be less so. If a youngster is depressed, it is important to know what kind of emergency care is available in your locality. (See chapter 4 for further discussion of the psychiatric emergency room.)

Crisis Services

Crisis services are usually components of a larger program (a hospital or a clinic) and may extend work that begins in an emergency room but continues after the initial visit. The availability of crisis services may determine whether a youngster goes into a hospital or can be treated in an outpatient setting.

If you feel a teenager is out of control, for whatever reason, the crisis team can go to your home and evaluate the situation. They call for backup from the police, and they have the authority to involuntarily hospitalize a youngster for evaluation and treatment in an emergency. The telephone number of the crisis team is an important number to have for the parents of a teenager in trouble.

Day Hospitals

Some hospitals and clinics offer care for patients who need more than the kind of care offered by outpatient clinics, but do not require hospitalizations. In addition, when a youngster is being discharged from a hospital, she may require a program before she is ready to return to school. Day hospitalization, sometimes called partial hospital programs, usually provides care that goes on for four or five hours a day, five days a week, and normally lasts no more than six to eight weeks. The patients will usually participate in a variety of group activities in addition to receiving individual treatment. These groups may focus on understanding the illness, improving social skills and functioning in school or at work, decreasing alcohol or other substance abuse, and controlling self-destructive impulses. For adolescents, there may be combined school and partial hospitalization programs until they are ready to return to school full-time.

A less intense version of this care is the intensive outpatient program, or IOP. This usually involves participation three to four days a week for treatment of specific illnesses such as eating disorders or chemical dependency as they relate to depression.

Adolescent Residential Care

Adolescent residential care is provided in facilities specifically designed to treat long-term psychiatric illness, including depression and self-destructive behaviors. These programs vary considerably in their philosophy and approach. Some involve families, some don't. Some are reimbursed by insurance, some may be paid for by the school system. They are generally very expensive, and insurance companies are reluctant to cover the cost.

In general, care should be provided to teenagers in the least restrictive facility that is safe and effective. If a youngster is mildly depressed or dysthymic but otherwise well functioning, then office-based psychiatric treatment is probably best. At the other extreme— if a youngster is suicidal, for example—the only proper treatment will involve hospitalization. But there are many choices along the continuum of care depending on the patient's physical health, her motivation to be in treatment, the severity of psychiatric illness, and the presence of other psychiatric problems (substance abuse, for example).

So much for definitions, since a definition alone is not enough to determine which therapist, or which facility, is best for a depressed teenager. How do you go about finding the right professional? A surprising number of people look for medical specialists in the Yellow Pages, but considering that the only requirement for being listed in the Yellow Pages is to have a business telephone line installed, this method is extremely unlikely to produce satisfactory results.

Referrals from other doctors or mental health professionals are the best place to begin. Ask your pediatrician, family physician, school counselor, or clergy member for a referral to a psychiatrist who has experience in treating adolescents. You may also contact a community hospital, state or county medical society, the Division of Child and Adolescent Psychiatry in any medical school or university, the American Psychiatric Association, or the American Academy of Child and Adolescent Psychiatry.

THE RIGHT THERAPIST

Even a therapist with the best training and qualifications in the world may not be the right therapist for a particular teenager. How can you tell who is right? Since successful therapy depends on trust between the therapist and the patient, this should be the first question you ask yourself: Is this a person we can trust, or is there something about him or her that makes us feel ill at ease? The answer will depend on the patient, but in figuring it out, most adolescents and their parents will find it helpful to ask some basic questions: Is the therapist responsive to our concerns? Does he seem to understand the difficulty we are having? Is her goal in treatment the same as ours? Do we agree with her approach to reaching these goals? On a practical level, is his office convenient, and can we afford the fee? Does it make a difference to us whether the therapist is a man or a woman?

Discussing these questions directly with the therapist is the best approach. Although a therapist may be reluctant to discuss his or her personal life, it can be useful for the teenager to figure out why the personal life of the therapist is important to him or her, and whether such considerations may stand in the way of successful treatment.

BEWARE OF THIS KIND OF THERAPIST

Major depression is a serious illness which usually requires medicine. Not all teenagers need medicine, and not all mental health practitioners prescribe it. As a parent or a teenager, you have the right to accept or reject any treatment, including medication. But if a mental health professional announces that he or she "doesn't believe in medicine," or actively disparages medical treatment for depression, this is someone to beware of. Using medicines to treat psychiatric illness is not a matter of belief. It is a matter of scientific research and scientific fact. A practitioner who rejects psychiatric medicine on principle is incapable of considering all the options for your teenager.

8

Medicine for Depression:
Pharmacological Treatments and
How They Work

In the early 1950s, the first medicine for mental illness was developed. It was called Thorazine, and it had the remarkable property of alleviating the terrifying hallucinations and irrational speech and behavior of people afflicted with schizophrenia. It didn't work for everyone, and even when it did work, it worked imperfectly and had many unpleasant side effects. But with all of its drawbacks, it was the only treatment for the disease that worked at all, and psychiatrists were of course delighted to be able to relieve, even if imperfectly, the symptoms of one of the most debilitating diseases known to mankind. The drug is still in wide use today. Once the usefulness of this drug was established, researchers began in earnest to develop other drugs to treat mental illness.

Most new drugs are developed by making modifications to the molecular structure of drugs already known. Researchers working on a tuberculosis treatment found that the drug they had synthesized—iproniazid, which interferes with the production of an enzyme called monoamine oxidase—did nothing for treating TB, but was effective in relieving the symptoms of depression. Thus, accidentally, the first antidepressant, a monoamine oxidase (MAO) inhibitor, was created. Researchers undertook modifications to the molecular structure of Thorazine in the hope of producing a better drug for schizophrenia, one more effective and with fewer side effects. The result was a drug called imipramine (brand name Tofranil). It was found to be ineffective for treating schizophrenia, but it did help in reducing depression. Thus imipramine became another fortuitous discovery, and another antidepressant. Imipramine was the first of a number of drugs developed thereafter that came to be known as "tricyclic antidepressants," named for the three-ring structure of their molecules. There are now about a dozen tricyclic antidepressants available for treating depression. Further research, and some other discoveries, produced more drugs for depression.

WHAT ANTIDEPRESSANTS DO

In the meantime, scientists were beginning to gain a more accurate understanding of how the brain works, which would lead to an understanding of the mechanisms of these drugs. It was widely known that nerves conduct electrical impulses, and that these electrical impulses pass from one nerve cell to another. But it turned out that this kind of electrical communication between nerve cells was only part of the story. In 1920, a Swiss researcher working with frog hearts figured out that the neurons of the vagus nerve (which controls, among other things, heartbeat) were producing a chemical in addition to an electrical charge. This chemical, later named acetylcholine, was the first neurotransmitter to be discovered. While the neuron was unquestionably producing an electric current, this "chemical synapse" between nerve cells turned out to be the way neurons communicate with each other.

The nerve cells in the brain—neurons—are not actually connected to one another. They are separated by about one-millionth of an inch, a space called the synaptic cleft. The place where neurons come together consists of a presynaptic ending that contains the neurotransmitters, a postsynaptic ending that has the receptor sites the neurotransmitter will attach to, and the synaptic cleft which is a small space between the neurons. This structure as a whole is called a synapse.

Nerves communicate when an electrical charge moves down the nerve along a structure called the axon and causes the release of chemicals by stimulating chemical-filled sacs, called vesicles, at the end of the neuron. These chemicals, the neurotransmitters, move across the synapse to the next neuron, where they attach to receptors whose structure permits only one kind of molecule to make the attachment—a kind of lock-and-key design. The drugs that treat depression (and other psychiatric illnesses) produce their effects by chemically altering the ability of these neurotransmitters to make their attachments and facilitate communication between neurons. More than fifty of these neurotransmitters have now been discovered, and they exist not only in the brain but in nerve cells all over the body. Moreover, there is now evidence that a neuron can release more than one kind of neurotransmitter.

All neurotransmitters, after being released and causing their biological effect, are then inactivated by one of three mechanisms. The chemical can drift away so that it stops attaching to the receptors on the next neuron (a process called diffusion). It can be broken down by an enzyme so that the receptor doesn't recognize it (enzymatic degradation). Or it can be reabsorbed into the axon terminal that released it, a process called "reuptake." Anything that interferes with these processes will cause changes in communication between nerves, and, if the change occurs in neurons in the brain, it can alter the way you feel. Scientists believe that both tricyclic antidepressants and MAO inhibitors cause the symptoms of depression to be alleviated by increasing the available amount of a neurotransmitter called norepinephrine. Tricyclic antidepressants also block the reuptake of another neurotransmitter called dopamine. Selective serotonin reuptake inhibitors (SSRIs), it is believed, affect the action of serotonin.

Of course, how antidepressants achieve their therapeutic effect is hypothesis, not proven fact, and there is probably no such thing as a drug that affects only one neurotransmitter without also altering other enzymes important in brain chemistry. The complex balance and interactions of these enzyme systems, and the complex effect drugs have on them, help explain why these medications have side effects as well as therapeutic effects, and why their impact on a given teenager will be to some degree unpredictable.

Categories of Antidepressants

Drugs are usually categorized by their chemical structure and their mechanisms of action. Among antidepressants, the three largest classes of drugs are tricyclics, monoamine oxidase (MAO) inhibitors, and SSRIs, but there are smaller classes as well, sometimes containing only one or two medications. A single drug often has more than one name: the generic name refers to its chemical compound, and the brand name is applied by a drug manufacturer to its pill or liquid version of that chemical. So, for instance, the first and most famous of the SSRIs, whose chemical name is fluoxetine, is usually referred to by its brand name, Prozac.

Therapeutic Effects of Antidepressants

We've explained what these drugs do physiologically in the brain. But what symptoms are actually relieved with antidepressants? At their best, antidepressants improve mood, relieve the physical symptoms of depression, such as fatigue and insomnia, and improve cognition so that the teenager experiences fewer irrationally hopeless thoughts. Because most antidepressants are also effective against anxiety, they will often relieve the symptoms of anxiety that frequently accompany depression. Since there are many different kinds of depression, some milder than others, you might think that lower doses would be required for milder cases of illness, but this isn't so. Treating dysthymia (the milder form of depression discussed in chapter 2) can require antidepressant doses just as high as those required for treating severe cases of major depression. Although there have been studies conducted to try to determine which antidepressants work best for which kinds of depression, there is still little evidence about this either for adults or teenagers.

When treating depression that includes psychotic symptoms such as delusions, or depression that could be part of bipolar disorder, it becomes even more important than in other forms of depression to be seeing a person with significant expertise in psychopharmacology and who understands the management of psychoses and mania. When depression is accompanied by psychosis, an antidepressant alone may not be sufficient, and it may be necessary to add an antipsychotic drug or to use electroconvulsive therapy (ECT). Delusional depression is a particularly serious form, since it has an increased rate of suicide. Depression has to be treated carefully in patients who have bipolar illness or are at risk for it because of family history. In such youngsters, it can be a delicate balancing act to treat the depression without precipitating mania. Sometimes this can be avoided by first treating the teenager with a mood stabilizer like lithium.

While antidepressants can be very helpful, they rarely solve the kinds of life problems that many depressed teenagers have—social difficulties with friends, inability to get along with parents, drug and alcohol abuse, and so on. Nor do they make up for periods of development that the teenager missed because of his illness. These issues are the province of psychotherapy and rehabilitation. Despite the improvements in cognition, many teens still continue to have negative thoughts about themselves, for which cognitive behavior therapy can be helpful. Psychodynamic psychotherapy can help address the relationship problems that remain after the medical treatment of depression. I never just give a pill and then let it go at that—figuring out what medicine to prescribe and in what doses it should be given is complex and essential, but there's more to good psychiatric care than writing prescriptions.

SIDE EFFECTS OF ANTIDEPRESSANTS

Tricyclics and MAO inhibitors have significant side effects and are generally not used with teenagers. In addition to their common tendency to cause dry mouth, nervousness, sedation, and weight gain, tricyclics can interfere with electrical impulses in the heart and are associated with a small number of unexplained deaths from cardiac events. The MAO inhibitors are impractical for use with teenagers because they require that certain food and drugs be avoided to prevent a potentially fatal reaction called a hypertensive crisis. Fortunately, several new classes of antidepressants are just as effective, usually have fewer and less troublesome side effects, and are available in many different variations so that youngsters and their doctors can find the one that works best. Prozac, one of the most widely prescribed drugs in the United States, is one of these.

Even with these new drugs, side effects are still a problem. Any antidepressant can precipitate a manic episode in certain people. Signs of incipient mania include hyperactivity, feelings of euphoria and grandiosity, sleeplessness without fatigue, and extreme irritability. Psychoactive drugs can also affect cognition, judgment, or motor activity, so people who take them should carefully assess how their performance is affected when they drive or operate hazardous machinery, and be sure that they can do so safely. Sometimes, for example, a person will drive a car more aggressively when an SSRI is started—teenagers should be made aware that this can happen, and that they must make the necessary adjustments. Antidepressants, like most drugs, should not be used during pregnancy unless absolutely necessary, since, although animal studies show no potential to harm a fetus, there is insufficient evidence about their effect on the human fetus. Some studies show that though SSRIs are secreted in breast milk, no detectable levels of the drug are found in the serum of infants. Postpartum depression is a dangerous and quite common illness; using SSRIs during breast feeding to combat it appears to be safe. Since, like most drugs, antidepressants are metabolized in the liver and excreted through the kidneys, patients with impaired liver or kidney function must be treated with caution. Some drugs are metabolized to a greater extent by the liver than the kidneys, and this may be one factor in selecting a drug if the teenager has a liver or kidney disorder.

In teenagers and young adults, perhaps the side effects that most commonly lead to discontinuation are the impaired sexual performance and weight gain that many of these drugs can cause.

It should also be noted that many of the commonly reported side effects of antidepressant medications are also symptoms of depression, so it is sometimes difficult to distinguish a side effect from a disease symptom. If a kid tells me that his medicine is giving him headaches, I have to try to figure out whether that's a side effect of the medicine or an effect of the depression—headaches are in fact a frequent symptom in depression. It would not be unexpected for a significant percentage of patients being treated for depression to report headaches no matter what drug they were taking, or even if they were taking no drug at all. For example, in a placebo-controlled clinical trial of Paxil, an SSRI, headaches were experienced by 17.6 percent of the people who took it—which sounds like a large number until you learn that 17.3 percent of the people who took the placebo also got headaches.

It is worth remembering that the longer a drug has been used, the more is known about its side-effect profile, both in short-term and especially in its long-term use. Although the side effects of the tricyclic antidepressants are fairly well known, we still have a lot to learn about those of the newer antidepressants. Often the longer you wait, the more bad news you learn. When I was in medical school, a professor of mine used to say, only half-jokingly, "Use a new drug quickly, while it still works."

FINDING THE RIGHT MEDICATION REGIMEN

Finding the right drug is often a question of trial and error. Psychotropic drugs can be difficult to prescribe effectively, partly because their biochemical action is not well understood and partly because there are so many individual reactions to different drugs and dosages. All drugs have side effects, some of which may not be tolerable, and there are many individual responses, both in feeling side effects and in getting relief from symptoms. A drug that works well for one person may not work at all for another. A drug may relieve a teenager's symptoms of depression but have side effects that make it impossible for her to take it. Effective dosage varies considerably from one person to another, and the dosage that achieves relief from symptoms may be very close to the dosage that causes intolerable side effects. Some people need very small doses, some much larger to achieve the same result. More experienced therapists are better at making the right estimates and adjustments—I know that I've grown better at it over the years.

The drugs don't work immediately, and their full beneficial effect may not be felt until they have been taken for weeks or even months. For some patients, the drugs do not work at all. All of this means that a psychiatrist must understand the actions of the drugs, know the predictable side effects, and inform the patient in detail of what to expect and when. And the psychiatrist must monitor her patients' progress carefully at all stages of treatment, making adjustments when necessary, and trying new medicines when one doesn't work. The discouraging thing is that a youngster may see side effects before he sees any relief from depression. But that doesn't mean the drug isn't working. Sometimes, even after an adequate length of time at an adequate dose, the first drug doesn't work, and then it may be necessary to try another. This period of trial and error can be frustrating. I constantly remind patients that they will feel better, and that we're going to work at it together until they feel completely well.

Varying effects and side effects must be carefully considered in finding the right medicine. Some kids will need a drug effective not only for depression but also for the anxiety that often accompanies it. Certain teenagers will feel better on antidepressants that are slightly sedating; others will need a more activating medicine. The severity of symptoms, the location of the treatment (whether the youngster is hospitalized or not), the question of suicidality—all of these factors are considered before I decide on the right medicine for a given teenager.

In order to minimize side effects and find the lowest effective dose, these drugs are usually started at lower doses and then increased as necessary over a period of time. I work with the patient to get the dose as low as possible while still maintaining effectiveness, but this is a delicate procedure. Reducing the drug too much, or too soon, can cause a relapse that may necessitate starting the process all over again.

As with any treatment regimen, the cooperation of the patient is essential. Even when antidepressants work well, they take time, and the teenager will have to be patient and persistent before he feels relief. Often the process goes quite smoothly, and the regimen requires little more of the youngster than listening to the occasional reminder to take the pill. But in other cases, the teenager may need to change dosages, vary the time of day he takes a medicine, try new drugs if the first one doesn't work, wait until unpleasant side effects subside. He will have to be conscientious about taking the medicine according to instructions, on a schedule that may have to be changed more than once to achieve the desired goal. The teenager will have to be his doctor's ally in finding the right treatment, and he will have to be convinced to continue taking the medicine after he feels better.

DOSING AND ADHERENCE

The dosing schedule of a given medicine can be a factor in which drug to choose because this can affect whether the medicine is taken regularly according to directions. Some drugs are cleared from the body faster than others. The faster a drug is cleared, the more frequently it needs to be taken to make sure that it is continuously present to exert its therapeutic effect. Some medicines can be taken either once a day or in divided dosages. In that case, usually once a day is best unless there are side effects that can be eliminated by spacing it out over the day.

Some drugs are available in slow release form, but there are teenagers who feel better when they space out the medicine. The longer a youngster has to stay on a drug, and the better she feels, the more likely she is to forget to take it—or to take it without even remembering that she took it. For this reason, I urge my patients to use a pill box that has a compartment for every day of the week so that they can set up a week's worth of medicine and then see at a glance whether they've taken today's dose. For best adherence, the simpler the schedule the better—and that's true for everyone, not just teenagers.

DRUG INTERACTIONS

Most drugs are broken down in the liver and then excreted by the kidneys. The liver has an enzyme system, called the cyctochrome P450 system, that has various pathways for this breakdown process. When a person is taking more than one drug, the drugs often compete for use of this system. As a result, the metabolism of either drug can be speeded up or slowed down. The prescribing physician must understand the direction of these effects, and increase or decrease doses of medication accordingly.

MAO inhibitors, separate from the issue of liver metabolism, can have bad interactions with many kinds of drugs, including possibly deadly reactions with other antidepressants. Asthma drugs, allergy medicine, diabetes medicines, medicines for high or low blood pressure, painkillers, mood stabilizers, sedatives, and stimulants can all have some ill effect, sometimes mild, sometimes dangerous, for a person on MAO inhibitors. Even excessive amounts of caffeine can cause blood pressure elevations, a racing heart, or anxiety in people taking MAO inhibitors (although moderate quantities are safe).

SSRIs have fewer bad drug interactions, but even here there are some. In addition to problems caused when they are combined with tricyclics (see page 177), SSRIs can cause problems when combined with antihistamines, diabetes medications, and heart and blood pressure drugs. Alcohol can cause increased drowsiness in people taking these pills, caffeine can cause excessive nervousness.

Tricyclics, which can be deadly if taken with MAO inhibitors, can have their toxicity increased by taking antibiotics, cause greater blood sugar decreases with diabetes medicines, and react badly with high and low blood pressure medicines, mood stabilizers, anticonvulsants, pain medications, sedatives, stimulants, and many other medicines. In addition to their many drug interactions, tricyclics can aggravate glaucoma, heart disease, liver disease, seizure disorders, and thyroid disease, so they must be used with extreme care in people suffering from such medical conditions.

Drug interaction is an extremely complex matter, and it must be discussed carefully with your doctor before you start any antidepressant.

ALCOHOL AND ILLICIT DRUGS

It is almost never a good idea to use alcohol or other recreational drugs when using antidepressants. Alcohol and other drugs can themselves cause the symptoms of depression and anxiety, both while they are being used and during withdrawal from them. They can also worsen the side effects of medications, for example, by causing increased sedation and changes in motor coordination, which can affect, among other things, the ability to drive a car safely. They can even modify the metabolism of a drug, making the dose prescribed incorrect. But telling a teenager (or even an adult) simply to avoid these things without telling him why or further discussing it, is usually futile. In fact, telling a teenager "don't drink alcohol with this medicine," and telling him nothing else, may result in the teen skipping the medicine in favor of the alcohol. It's important when a teenager is being treated for depression that the physician have a sense of how to talk honestly with him about alcohol and drug use, and to address the fact that these substances can make his problems worse. These are important discussions that the physician must undertake with great skill, the utmost seriousness, and with absolute assurances of confidentiality.

When reading about any of the drugs described later in this chapter, be aware that both safety and efficacy are enhanced with all of them if the youngster avoids alcohol and recreational drugs.

PHASES OF MEDICATION TREATMENT

There are two parts to the drug treatment of depression, the acute phase and the maintenance phase. The first involves the trial-and-error process described above, where an effective and tolerable regimen is worked out. The maintenance phase is the continuation of that regimen to prevent relapse—that is, a return of the depressive symptoms. Medication is not a cure, and depression can recur when the medication is stopped. The more frequent previous depression episodes have been, the more likely relapse is to occur.

Stopping SSRIs too abruptly can cause a collection of symptoms called "discontinuation syndrome." The main symptoms include dizziness and lack of muscle coordination. Nausea and vomiting, and flulike symptoms of fatigue, lethargy, muscle pain, and chills can also occur. Some people complain of sensory disturbances such as tingling sensations. Sleep disturbances can also happen, with insomnia and/or extremely vivid dreams. The psychological symptoms associated with discontinuation syndrome are anxiety, agitation, crying spells, and irritability. Overactivity, depersonalization (the experience of oneself as detached, as if you were an outside observer), decreased concentration, lowered mood, and confusion and memory problems can also occur. These symptoms are more common with Paxil and Zoloft, and not common with Prozac because the body takes so long to clear Prozac from the system after ceasing to take it. In any case, it is almost always a bad idea to stop any antidepressant abruptly just because the bottle is empty. Gradually tapering the medicine reduces the likelihood of unpleasant physical reactions or the return of psychiatric symptoms.

Many teenagers will say "If I feel better, why should I be taking a pill?" But stopping an antidepressant too early can be a terrible mistake. Once an antidepressant becomes effective, I will keep a patient on the medicine for at least six months before even thinking of beginning to taper it off, and even longer if there has been more than one episode of depression or if the depression was a longstanding and chronic problem.

Parents, too, may feel pressure to get their teenager off a medicine even when the medicine is working well and there are no side effects. There are powerful psychological reasons for this. After all, if the youngster isn't taking any medicine, that means he's no longer sick. It means that it might never happen again, or that it wasn't all that serious in the first place. Parents don't want to believe that their teenager has an illness, especially a psychiatric illness, because they feel, quite wrongly, that it somehow reflects badly on them. Getting off the medicine, they feel, will take care of that problem. But these feelings must be resisted, both because they are unjustified, and because there is nothing more discouraging than stopping a medicine, seeing the symptoms reappear, and then having to start all over again to get the symptoms under control.

A NEW SPECIALTY

The use of psychotropic medicines is so complex that a new subspecialty—psychopharmacology—has appeared, and some psychiatrists, called psychopharmacologists, now limit their practice to therapy with these medicines. At the same time, because the newer drugs are relatively safe (they don't do much harm even if they are misused), because they have an easy dosing schedule, and because they have been extensively marketed to many other specialists, including general practitioners, they are now widely prescribed by many doctors besides psychiatrists. The problem is that even when general practitioners diagnose depression correctly (often they overlook it) they may prescribe ineffectively: they give doses that are too small, they don't persist long enough with the regimen, they fail to try different drugs when one isn't working. They are not always familiar with side effects and how to manage them and therefore don't necessarily inform the patient properly about them. Sometimes they are not available to monitor a patient's response as often as may be necessary. Despite the new, easy-to-use medicines, prescribing for depression is much more difficult than prescribing, say, a course of antibiotics for a strep throat. It is obviously cheaper to have a family doctor prescribe for depression, and there are economic forces that would like to see this become standard practice. But studies have found that the medicines are more effective when prescribed and monitored by a specialist—that is, by a psychiatrist—and that psychotropic drugs prescribed by nonspecialists may be a bad bargain. A specialist is best equipped to tailor a regimen that promises the best possible results for a given teenager. You wouldn't ask a psychiatrist to prescribe medicine for high blood pressure; why ask an internist or a general practitioner to prescribe antidepressants?

DRUG SAFETY AND EFFECTIVENESS

The Food and Drug Administration requires that a drug be shown to be both safe and effective before it approves it for sale. This is a complex process that usually requires a drug company to carry out years of extremely expensive studies and clinical tests on a given drug before they can bring it to market. The FDA further requires that the drug company list the specific "indications" for which the drug is approved—that is, the uses for which enough scientific evidence has been gathered to show the drug would work for that problem. These tests—and this is true for all drugs, not just the psychiatric medicines we discuss here—don't usually involve testing the drugs specifically on teenagers, so the FDA approves most drugs for use by adults only. Strictly speaking, most of the new antidepressants are not approved by the FDA for use in teenagers—that is, large clinical studies have not been carried out on these drugs that specifically focus on depressed people under the age of 18. But doctors in clinical practice are free both ethically and legally to use approved drugs as they see fit, and these medicines, like many nonpsychiatric medicines, are widely and safely used among teenagers, and with considerable success.

Drug companies are, of course, eager to find new uses for their drugs, and after a drug is marketed for one purpose, often a company will pursue approval for other uses. Several of the SSRIs are now FDA-approved for treating not only depression but also panic disorder, obsessive-compulsive disorder (OCD), and other illnesses. These approvals often come after physicians have been using the drugs for these purposes for some time because they have found them clinically effective, which may then lead the drug company to conduct the formal scientific studies required for FDA approval.

FDA approval is not only difficult and expensive, but in some ways also controversial. Drug companies naturally want to see their drugs approved for as many purposes as possible—approvals promise more sales and more profits. For the same economic reasons, drug companies also want to invent new drugs that they can hold exclusive licenses to produce (these patents expire after a certain period of time, and then anyone can produce the drug). Pharmaceutical companies, therefore, have considerable motivation to get people to use their patented drugs rather than the possibly equally effective remedies that are commonly available and not exclusively owned by anyone. Drug companies aggressively promote their patented drugs, both to doctors and (within limits imposed by the FDA) directly to patients. Some people cite this drug company hard sell as one of the reasons doctors steer people away from cheaper remedies in favor of expensive pills. They may be partly correct, but the story is more complicated than that.

The fact is that FDA approval, though it aids the drug companies in pursuit of their goals, gives the physician and the patient something valuable, too: the assurance that carefully designed scientific studies have shown that the medicines they are taking will not harm them and will actually work in the ways promised. The approval process also provides essential information on dosages and drug interactions, and the assurance that the drug is manufactured according to procedures that assure strength and purity. Drug manufacturers may be venal, they may be more concerned with profits than health, but even granting that these things are true, the procedures the FDA insists they follow before being permitted to sell a drug assure the availability of scientific information that is invaluable.

In addition to the research that goes on before a drug is sold, the FDA gathers post-marketing information on adverse drug reactions. This is important because many more people are exposed to a drug after it is marketed, so that dangerous side effects that are rare, or that only occur after the drug is used for an extended period of time, can be discovered. These reports may change recommendations for using the drug, or even result in a drug being withdrawn from the market completely. (When a drug is taken off the market, it is widely assumed that this means the FDA "made a mistake." This is not necessarily so. That a drug is taken off the market may mean, on the contrary, that the system the FDA has set up is working properly.) This kind of information about safety, efficacy, and purity is not available for other substances (herbal remedies, for example), however useful a patient may find them. Most psychiatrists shy away from recommending such remedies precisely for this reason—there isn't enough scientific information about them.

New drugs are often expensive. Insurance companies may not cover them, or cover only part of the cost. Many drug companies have programs to cover the cost of drugs for people who could not otherwise afford them, and if you are in this position, giving the drug company a call (there is almost always an 800 number) can be worth the effort.

SSRIs

The SSRIs have become widely used for two very good reasons: they are effective, and they are easy to prescribe safely. The older tricyclics and MAO inhibitors, discussed below, can be just as effective in relieving symptoms as the selective serotonin reuptake inhibitors. They are, however, much more toxic in overdose and have many more unpleasant side effects, so most physicians and patients now prefer to use the newer antidepressants as the first choice. A given SSRI may work for one person and not for another, and the various drugs in this group vary slightly in effects and side effects. Yet because they are similar in chemical structure, certain generalizations apply to all of them. After the first of these medicines, fluoxetine, whose brand name is Prozac, was established as an effective SSRI, the search was on to find SSRIs that were more effective and had fewer side effects (and, to be sure, to find a drug as financially successful as Prozac). It wasn't long before four more SSRIs appeared on the market; Zoloft (sertraline), Paxil (paroxetine), Luvox (fluvoxamine), and Celexa (citalopram).

The SSRIs act to prevent the postsynaptic vesicles from reabsorbing a particular neurotransmitter—serotonin—thereby making more of the chemical available in the brain. This action is believed to be responsible for relieving the symptoms of depression, and in some cases these medicines do that almost miraculously. A teenager must understand that she may not see significant improvement in her symptoms until four to six weeks after starting an SSRI. But I have often observed that while teenagers started on SSRIs may not get better quickly, they usually do not get worse. In short, the drugs are worth the effort involved in taking them.

None of the SSRIs should be taken with the antihistamine Hismanal (astemizole), and the potential for drug interactions increases with higher dosages. Some patients on SSRIs complain of mild cognitive changes—some forgetfulness, or a tendency to reverse digits in a telephone number, for example.

The most common side effects of these drugs are headache, nervousness, and insomnia. Although the literature says little about it, it is overwhelmingly clear to all physicians who have prescribed SSRIs that they interfere with sexual performance. In a certain percentage of men, this takes the form of delayed orgasm. In women, they may make orgasm difficult or impossible. In larger doses, they can cause diminution of sexual desire. As with other side effects, lowering the dosage can help.

The SSRIs have various other side effects in common. The most frequent are drowsiness, initial loss of appetite, headaches, stomach upset, diarrhea, or constipation, and, possibly, long-term weight gain. Some of these side effects are temporary—if a patient can tolerate them for a time, they often just go away. Some side effects are dose related—unfortunately, for some teenagers by the time they get up to a dose that helps the depression, the side effects become intolerable.

The SSRIs that have been around the longest—Prozac, for example—show no adverse effects when used over long periods of time, even over many years. But there are few scientific studies of the effects of these medicines over long periods of time, and there is no assurance that negative effects will not develop with continued use.

One of the great advantages of SSRIs over the older antidepressants is that their side effects are much more tolerable and result in more people continuing to use the drug. A recent study, for example, found that though Prozac was no more effective in treating depression than the tricyclic imipramine, only 14 percent of those on Prozac dropped out of the study, while 34 percent of those on imipramine dropped out (and 23 percent of those taking a placebo). No matter how effective a medicine may be, it won't work if the side effects are so unpleasant that the youngster won't take it.

Prozac (Fluoxetine)

Prozac, a drug whose fame is now approaching notoriety, was the first selective serotonin reuptake inhibitor. In addition to relieving depression, Prozac is also effective as one component of the treatment of bulimia and obsessive-compulsive disorder.

Prozac can be taken with or without food, in one daily dose. It is metabolized (that is, degraded and eliminated from the body) by the liver, but one of the things the liver turns it into—norfluoxetine—is also a serotonin reuptake inhibitor, which degrades more slowly than Prozac itself. This gives the drug a long duration of action, and after you stop taking Prozac, its effects persist for a considerable length of time—as long as five weeks. Reports of death due to overdose of Prozac have been rare, and even in large overdoses (as many as a hundred of the typical 20 mg pills), there are rarely lasting adverse effects.

Many drugs can cause a rash, and so can Prozac, but since Prozac stays in the body so long, a rash caused by it can be troublesome. Drug rashes can lead to more serious medical complications, so if a rash develops, it usually means that the Prozac should be stopped.

The dosage of Prozac varies considerably from one person to another. For patients with depression, as little as 5 mg or as much as 80 mg a day can be effective. Most patients start with 20 mg once a day, and the dose is adjusted up or down from there. Much higher dosages are required for treating obsessive-compulsive disorder and bulimia.

In studies, about 15 percent of people who take Prozac discontinue it because of some adverse event. These most commonly include headache, nervousness, insomnia, or fatigue, and, more rarely, anxiety, dry mouth, stomach upset, eating problems, and excessive sweating.

Prozac is sold in 10 mg and 20 mg tablets, and in a liquid form. It is also available in 10 mg caplets that are scored so they can be easily broken in half. Since the spring of 2001, a once-a-week dosage has been available that causes less gastric upset but can only be used when the patient has been on the same dose for at least three months.

Zoloft (Sertraline)

Zoloft is approved not only for treating depression but for obsessive-compulsive disorder and panic disorder as well. Many physicians use it for treating eating disorders, too, although it is not FDA-approved for this purpose. One advantage it may have over Prozac is that it clears from the system more quickly after being discontinued, which may be helpful in certain situations.

Zoloft is usually taken once a day, and the starting dose is 25 mg to 50 mg. Usually the doctor will gradually increase the dosage up to 100 or 150 mg. Going up to 200 mg is acceptable. It helps to take Zoloft with food, since having some food in your stomach increases your ability to absorb the medicine.

Zoloft has few drug interactions, though one that should be noted is with cimetidine, the active ingredient in Tagamet and other antacid medicines. Cimetidine may decrease the absorption of Zoloft and thereby minimize its usefulness.

In the clinical studies that preceded its introduction, the side effects of Zoloft that affected more than 2 percent of the patients were nausea, diarrhea, upset stomach, male sexual dysfunction (ejaculatory delay), insomnia and somnolence, tremor, sweating, dry mouth, and dizziness. Of these, dry mouth, headache, and nausea were the most common.

Zoloft comes in 50 mg and 100 mg tablets, both of them scored so that they can be broken into half doses.

Paxil (Paroxetine)

Paxil is yet another SSRI, with a slightly different chemical structure and slightly different dosage and side effects, but with similar antidepressant action. It is approved for use in panic disorder and obsessive-compulsive disorder as well. Some patients need much smaller doses of Paxil than others to get the same results. The initial dose is 20 mg once a day, and it can be increased by 10 mg at intervals of one or two weeks up to 50 mg a day. Unlike Zoloft, Paxil's absorption isn't increased by taking it with food.

The most commonly observed side effects of Paxil are headache, nausea, somnolence, sweating, tremor, weakness, dizziness, dry mouth, insomnia, and male sexual dysfunction (mainly ejaculatory delay). In one study, 12.9 percent of men who took the drug experienced delayed ejaculation, while no one who took the placebo did. Not all men view delayed ejaculation as an undesirable side effect, and in fact Paxil is sometimes used as a treatment for premature ejaculation. Suffice it to say that Paxil has certain side effects including some that can be serious, but most are minor, uncommon, or both.

Paxil comes in 10 mg, 20 mg, 30 mg, and 40 mg tablets.

Luvox (Fluvoxamine)

Luvox has FDA approval only for treating obsessive-compulsive disorder, but many psychiatrists find it useful for treating depression as well. This drug has been tested in children and adolescents—but only for its effect on OCD, not depression. (It is more effective in treating OCD in children than in teenagers.)

Luvox, supplied in 50 mg and 100 mg tablets, is usually started at 50 mg once a day at bedtime, then increased gradually as tolerated until the desired effect is achieved. The maximum dosage is 300 mg. Doses above 150 mg should be divided, with a maximum of 150 mg at bedtime.

Celexa (Citalopram)

As of this writing, Celexa is the most recently available SSRI in the United States. Citalopram, its active ingredient, is a highly selective inhibitor of serotonin reuptake. It seems to have little or no effect on other neurotransmitters.

Celexa is taken once a day, and its effectiveness is not changed by food, so you can take it any time. The most common reason why people stopped taking the drug in the clinical trials was nausea; somewhat less common reasons were insomnia and somnolence.

SEROTONIN ANTAGONISTS

While an SSRI prevents the reuptake of serotonin when it is released at the synapse, this group of drugs produces their effect by binding to the neurotransmitters themselves. These drugs probably inhibit the reuptake of serotonin and norepinephrine, but their chemical structure is unlike that of any of the SSRIs, tricyclics, or MAO inhibitors, and they act on different serotonin receptor sites.

Serzone (Nefazodone)

There are some interactions of Serzone with other drugs: it potentiates the effect of the anti-anxiety drugs Halcion or Xanax by raising plasma levels, so dosages of those drugs must be reduced or eliminated when using Serzone. It should never be taken with Propulsid (an antacid).

The most common side effects are nausea, dizziness, insomnia, muscle weakness, and agitation. Sometimes people who take Serzone experience dizziness if they stand up too quickly. Sexual side effects occur, but less frequently than with SSRIs. Dry mouth, drowsiness, constipation, and blurred vision occur more rarely. When the drug first came out, the starting dose was 200 mg per day in two doses, but in practice that has been found to be a bit high. The drug is now usually started at 50 mg twice a day. The dosage must be raised gradually—no more often than once a week, 100 mg per day each time. Doses up to 600 mg a day can be used. Serzone is available in 100 mg, 150 mg, 200 mg, and 250 mg pills, and the 100 mg and 150 mg pills are scored so they can be broken in half. The advantages of Serzone over other antidepressants are the lower incidence of sexual side effects and disturbed sleep.

Desyrel (Trazodone)

Desyrel inhibits the reuptake of serotonin, but it is chemically unrelated to any other antidepressant. It is effective for treating depression alone and, like Serzone, also effective for relieving depression with anxiety. Many psychiatrists prefer not to prescribe this medicine for men because of a rare but serious side effect: priapism, or prolonged or inappropriate erections which may necessitate surgical intervention and can result in permanent failure of erectile function and impotence.

Having food in your stomach helps in absorption of the drug, so it is advisable to take it after a meal or snack. In clinical trials, the most common side effects were drowsiness, dry mouth, and dizziness. Trazodone is so likely to cause drowsiness that it is often used in very low doses (doses too low to have an antidepressant effect) as a sleep aid. It is nonaddictive and, unlike other sleep medicines, you don't develop resistance to it, so larger doses are never required and it can be used over long periods of time.

Trazodone is started at lower doses and increased gradually. Larger doses are often taken at bedtime. The initial dose is 150 mg a day divided into two or three doses, and this can be gradually increased to attain the proper relief up to 400 mg per day for outpatients. More severely depressed inpatients may take as much as 600 mg per day.

MORE NEW ANTIDEPRESSANTS

In addition to the SSRIs and the serotonin antagonists, three other drugs are now available that, by their chemical structure, don't fit into either group but nevertheless have similar beneficial effects.

Effexor (Venlafaxine)

Effexor was introduced to the American market in 1993, and it is sometimes called an SNRI—serotonin and norepinephrine reuptake inhibitor—since it acts on both of these neurotransmitters. It also inhibits dopamine, somewhat less strongly. Food doesn't affect the absorption of the drug, so you can take it with or without a meal.

Effexor cannot be used with MAO inhibitors, but it seems to have less potential for drug interactions than the other antidepressants, since it is only a weak inhibitor of enzymes in the liver that break down other drugs.

One of the possible side effects of Effexor is an increase in blood pressure, so anyone on the drug should have regular blood pressure checks to make sure this doesn't become a problem. In a minority of patients, the drug can cause anxiety, nervousness, and insomnia. There isn't any evidence that the drug affects cognitive or psychomotor performance of otherwise healthy people, but the precautions mentioned above for all antidepressants should be followed anyway.

About 6 percent of people who try Effexor experience nausea severe enough to make them stop taking it. Three percent of people who take it will have to discontinue because of headaches, insomnia, or dizziness; a smaller percentage stop because of nervousness, dry mouth, excessive sweating, or anxiety. As in clinical studies with other antidepressants, about 25 percent get headaches on Effexor, and so do 24 percent of those who take the placebo. On the other hand, 37 percent of the people in this study on Effexor felt nauseated, while only 11 percent of those on the placebo did. As people take the drug longer, some side effects, especially dizziness and nausea, diminish.

Effexor is available in two forms: immediate release, which must be taken two or three times a day, and Effexor XR, which is a sustained-release capsule that can be taken once a day. With the immediate-release form, the usual starting dose is 75 mg divided into two or three portions, and the dosage can be gradually increased up to 225 mg a day to achieve effectiveness. For some of the most severely depressed patients, doses up to 375 mg a day, divided into three portions, have proven effective. The pills come in five different sizes from 25 mg to 100 mg.

Wellbutrin (Bupropion)

Wellbutrin weakly inhibits the reuptake of serotonin, norepinephrine, and dopamine. Although it is approved only for treating depression, I've used it successfully with adolescents for treating attention-deficit disorder. It is somewhat activating and therefore useful for teenagers who feel slowed down either by the depression itself or by the side effects of other antidepressants. (For the same reason, some youngsters will feel too anxious on it.) Wellbutrin has one severe side effect that the other newer drugs do not seem to have: it can cause seizures at higher doses, usually at doses that exceed the recommended levels. This doesn't happen often—in about 0.4 percent, or 13 of 3,200 patients in one study—but it happens often enough to warrant a caution about its use, and to avoid it completely in patients with seizure disorders.

Wellbutrin is available in two forms, an immediate-release form which comes in 75 mg and 100 mg tablets, and a sustained-release form in 100 mg and 150 mg tablets. In the immediate-release form, doses can range from 75 mg to 100 mg taken twice a day. In the sustained-release form, it can be given as 150 mg taken once a day in the morning. If all goes well, the dose can be increased up to 300 mg within a week. The 300 mg are taken in two doses of 150 mg, separated by at least eight hours. The maximum dose for the sustained-release form is 400 mg.

Wellbutrin—or rather, bupropion, its active ingredient—is also approved as an aid in smoking cessation, and may have an anti-smoking effect in teenagers who smoke cigarettes. When the company advertises and sells it for this purpose, however, it changes the name to Zyban. (If you listen closely to the TV ads for Zyban, a voiceover cautions not to take Zyban if you are taking Wellbutrin—good advice, since it is exactly the same medicine!) To be sure, the drug is used in different dosages and on a different schedule for smoking cessation, and this may be one reason to give it another brand name. But perhaps the company also believes that the stigma of taking a "mental illness medicine" would discourage people from buying Wellbutrin only to help them quit smoking. (You will usually have to pay a few dollars more for a bottle of Zyban than for an absolutely identical bottle of sustained-release Wellbutrin. An Internet site I checked sells Zyban in the 150 mg sustained-release form for $120, and the same 100 tablets as Wellbutrin for $116.) Interestingly, many insurance companies will not cover the cost of bupropion for smoking cessation, but they will if it's for depression.

Remeron (Mirtazapine)

Besides affecting serotonin and other neurotransmitters, Remeron is a potent antagonist of histamine, which probably explains why it makes some kids sleepy. In fact, more than half the people who take it experience this drowsiness. Other side effects include dry mouth, increased appetite, weight gain, dizziness, and constipation. Less common side effects include abnormal dreams, tremors, and agranulocytosis (a potentially serious condition that interferes with the production of white blood cells, limiting the body's ability to fight infection). If your white blood cell count decreases on the drug, you have to stop taking it, but this happens only to about 1 in 1,000 people who take it, and it is usually reversible if the drug is stopped.

Remeron comes in 15 mg and 30 mg tablets, and the starting dose is 15 mg at bedtime. This is increased gradually, raising the dosage over a period of weeks up to 45 mg a day in a single dose.

How effective is it? At least as effective as Prozac and the other SSRIs. One big advantage of it is that it rarely affects sexual function, a problem that can be severe with the SSRIs. Because it is a sedative, it is a useful drug for people who suffer from insomnia along with their depression. It is very helpful in reducing anxiety as well, so much so that it has been used successfully to reduce preoperative anxiety in surgical patients.

TRICYCLIC ANTIDEPRESSANTS

Tricyclics, named for the three-ring structure of their molecules, are now rarely used for teenagers. One of the first antidepressants ever developed, imipramine, is a tricyclic, and there are seven others as well. They each have slightly different effects and side effects; some work well for some patients and not at all for others. Before the newer antidepressants were developed, tricyclics were the best medicine for depression and teenagers used them before the development of SSRIs and other medications. There may be a small number of adolescents who can still benefit from their use, but I rarely prescribe them.

Tricyclics are as effective as SSRIs and the other newer drugs, but their side effects remain a problem. They range from the common and annoying to the rare and fatal, and almost everyone who takes tricyclics experiences some unwanted side effect at one time or another. In milder cases of depression, the side effects can be so bad that they are experienced as worse than the symptoms of the illness, making the drugs virtually useless. If they are used for suicidal kids, it must be with supervision in which someone keeps the medication safely locked away—as little as a two-week's supply can be fatal in overdose. For many tricyclics, it is possible to obtain blood levels of the medication in order to determine if the dosage is in the clinical range. This helps in selecting the lowest possible dosage and minimizing side effects.

Tricyclics have withdrawal symptoms, too. If they are taken for a long time in high doses and then abruptly stopped, they can cause nausea, vomiting, or diarrhea. This is particularly true for amitriptyline, imipramine, clomipramine, trimipramine, and doxepin. Tricyclic antidepressants should be used with extreme caution in patients with a preexisting seizure disorder because the seizure threshold may be lowered. Tricyclics (like many other drugs) should be discontinued several days before elective surgery.

Tricyclics increase the effect of anticholinergic drugs—drugs containing atropine or epinephrine, for example. These include many different drugs used as decongestants and local anesthetics. People using these drugs along with tricyclics may require smaller doses of anticholinergics (and larger doses if they stop using those drugs).

Those with Parkinson's disease or respiratory depression—not likely disorders in kids—have to use tricyclics carefully. Cardiac disease is also rare in teenagers, but since there are adverse cardio-vascular effects associated with tricyclics, anyone with cardiac dis-ease should use them with great caution, even though the serious adverse events are more likely to occur after acute overdose. Tri-cyclic antidepressants should not be given to patients who are in the acute recovery phase following a heart attack, again an extreme rarity in an adolescent. It may be useful to obtain a baseline electro-cardiogram, since some tricyclics will cause changes in heart rhythm and rate. Asthma, which is a common problem in teenagers, can be aggravated by tricyclic antidepressants.

Tricyclics can be given along with SSRIs, although this is usually not done. If they are used together, they must be used with caution because the two drugs compete with each other for the liver enzymes that metabolize them and eliminate them from the body.

If a teenager is on a tricyclic antidepressant, he or she has to be careful of sunburn. Wearing a hat and long-sleeved clothing and applying a sunblock is a good idea. Thyroid drugs can accelerate the response to tricyclic antidepressants, and using them with thyroid drugs can cause cardiac arrhythmias. They should be used with cau-tion in such patients. People taking antihistamines or cimetidine (the active ingredient in Tagamet) also need to use tricyclics with caution.

Tofranil (Imipramine)

Imipramine was approved for use by the FDA in 1959. Tofranil was the original brand name, but the drug is now available under the brand name SK-Pramine and under its generic name. No one is quite sure how it works, but the most common hypothesis is that it blocks the uptake of norepinephrine at the nerve synapses.

The adult dose of imipramine is initially 50 mg per day in divided doses, usually increased gradually up to 200 mg as needed. As much as 300 mg per day can be given. In adolescents, however, an initial dose of 25 mg is normally used, and it is rarely necessary to increase the dosage above 100 mg per day to achieve the desired effect. Imipramine is available in many different pill sizes.

Elavil (Amitriptyline)

Amitriptyline, first approved by the FDA as an antidepressant in 1961, is now available in generic formulations under many different brand names including Endep, Etrafon, Limbitrol, and Triavil (under this last name it is combined with another drug, perphenazine) as well as under the generic name amitriptyline. Amitriptyline has sedative effects in addition to antidepressant effects.

The pills come in 10 mg, 25 mg, 50 mg, 75 mg, 100 mg, and 150 mg. For adolescents, the recommended doses are 10 mg three times a day, with 20 mg at bedtime. (Such a dosing schedule may prove unrealistic for most teenagers). Because of its sedative effect, larger doses are usually taken at bedtime, smaller ones during the day.

Anafranil (Clomipramine)

Although Anafranil is officially approved only for treating obsessive-compulsive disorder, it is sometimes used in lower doses for depression, and as a treatment for panic attacks and anxiety. Weight gain is a common side effect of using the drug, and in some patients the weight gain can be as high as 25 percent of initial body weight. It is sedating, so the starting dose of 25 mg is usually given at bedtime. This dose can be increased as tolerated and given in divided doses up to 250 mg. At higher doses, there can be an increase in blood pressure, which will require monitoring. Anafranil is one of the few psychiatric medicines that has been tested in and is specifically approved for use with adolescents, but still, its side effects make it problematic for teens.

Norpramin (Desipramine)

Prior to the development of the newer classes of antidepressants, Norpramin, also sold under the brand name Pertofrane, was the tricyclic most often used for adolescents because it isn't overly sedating and is not associated with significant weight gain. Adolescent doses usually start at 25 mg daily and can be increased up to 150 mg either in a single dose or divided doses. Dosages up to 300 mg a day can be used.

Sinequan (Doxepin)

Sinequan is also available under the brand name Adapin and the generic name doxepin. Tagamet potentiates the effects and side effects of Sinequan and should not be taken with it. Tagamet is a histamine receptor antagonist, and so is Sinequan. This property is probably what makes Sinequan effective in a topically applied cream form (the brand name is Zonalon) as a treatment for the rashes caused by eczema and other allergies. When Sinequan is used as a topical cream, it can have many of the same effects as when it is taken orally in pill form, so the same cautions and warnings apply, and dosages of tricyclics should usually be reduced if the cream is being used concomitantly.

As an antidepressant, a dosage of 75 mg to 150 mg of Sinequan per day is recommended, but doses up to 300 mg a day can be used for patients who do not respond to lower amounts. The medicine can be taken once a day or in divided doses. When one dose a day is taken, it is usually 150 mg a day taken at bedtime (the medicine is a sedative and in fact is sometimes used in small doses for insomnia). The 150 mg single daily dose is only for maintenance therapy and not recommended as the initial dose. Sinequan comes in six different pill sizes ranging from 10 mg to 150 mg, and in a liquid solution.

Pamelor (Nortriptyline)

Nortriptyline is now available under the brand names Aventyl and Pamelor, as well as under its generic name. The usual tricyclic precautions apply, and it can also, though rarely, cause seizures. Cimetidine (Tagamet), like alcohol, can potentiate the effects of Pamelor.

Adolescents usually require a slightly lower dose than adults, but the usual starting dose is 25 mg. This can be increased gradually up to 150 mg per day, but doses larger than that are not recommended.

Vivactil (Protriptyline)

Vivactil is used for all types of depression. Sometimes it causes insomnia, so it may be given along with a sedating agent to counteract this tendency.

The usual side effects of tricyclics apply to Vivactil as well: it can cause stomach upset, increased appetite and weight gain, temporary confusion in high doses, and, rarely, hallucinations. The drowsiness that sometimes occurs when people start Vivactil usually disappears as the therapy is continued.

Generally speaking, the correct dosage for adolescents is 5 mg three times a day—again, a difficult regimen to follow—with gradual increases as necessary, usually adding to the dose taken in the morning. Vivactil comes in 5 mg and 10 mg tablets.

Surmontil (Trimipramine)

Surmontil is useful in treating all types of depression. Adolescents will usually start with a dose of 50 mg, with gradual increases up to 100 mg to achieve the desired effect. The drug is available in 25 mg, 50 mg, and 100 mg pills.

TETRACYCLIC ANTIDEPRESSANTS

In the hope of producing an antidepressant with fewer unpleasant side effects than the tricyclics, drug researchers altered their molecules to produce two tetracyclic antidepressants, so named because their molecule has four rings instead of three (Greek tetra = four). But it didn't turn out as well as hoped, and these tetracyclic antidepressants actually work the same way, and have many of the same side effects, as the tricyclics. Still, certain people will find relief, and fewer side effects, with one of the tetracyclics.

Amoxapine

Amoxapine (available now in generic form—the old brand name was Asendin) presents certain unique risks, risks that make me hesitate to use the drug when there are so many other antidepressants available. First, it is much more likely than other cyclics to cause seizures. Second, because it blocks dopamine receptors, like many antipsychotic drugs such as Thorazine, it can cause some of the same side effects that those drugs cause: galactorrhea in women (inappropriate production of breast milk), and akathesia, a kind of muscular restlessness that makes you unable to sit still. This is uncomfortable, but not dangerous. Although it happens rarely, it can also cause symptoms like those of Parkinson's disease—tremor, stiffness, and stooped posture. These go away when you stop using the drug, but no one who experiences these side effects should continue taking it.

Another rare, but much more serious, side effect is tardive dyskinesia, a neurological disorder that causes involuntary movement of the lips and tongue, and sometimes the arms and legs. Tardive dyskinesia is difficult to treat even after the drug is stopped, and it may never go away completely. Finally, the drug can also cause, very rarely, something called neuroleptic malignant syndrome, or NMS. This is characterized by high fever, cardiac abnormalities, blood pressure changes, delirium, and muscle rigidity. It can be fatal.

Most psychiatrists would use amoxapine only when other drugs have failed, and rarely with a teenager. Starting with 50 mg twice a day, the dosage can be increased to 50 mg three times a day in a few days. Higher doses should be used only after excluding a history of convulsive disorders, but doses up to 400 mg or more a day have been used successfully with some patients.

Maprotiline

Maprotiline, formerly known as Ludiomil and now available only in generic form, inhibits the reuptake of noradrenaline, but not serotonin. It has a sedative effect on the anxiety that can accompany depression. The most common side effects are dry mouth, sleepiness, blurred vision, constipation, and nervousness but most side effects of maprotiline are mild and transient. They usually disappear with continued therapy or with dose reduction.

The recommendation is to start at 75 mg a day in two or three divided doses, then increase gradually, 25 mg as tolerated, beginning after two weeks on this regimen. The maximum dose is 150 mg a day. Higher doses increase the risk of seizure.

MAO INHIBITORS

Monoamine oxidase (MAO) is the name of a complex enzyme system that is widely distributed throughout the body, and drugs that inhibit the action of this system cause various clinical effects. It isn't clear whether the antidepressant effect of the MAO inhibitors comes from MAO inhibition itself, from some other effect the drug has, or from a combination of effects. In any case, the action of MAO inhibitors is slightly different from that of other antidepressants. They seem to increase the amount of neurotransmitters released by the nerve endings, rather than limiting their reuptake at the synapse. These drugs are extremely rare in the treatment of teenagers for a variety of reasons, the most important being the diet restrictions which are almost impossible for teenagers to follow.

The most important warnings with these drugs involve food and other prescription and over-the-counter medications. The MAO inhibitors cannot be taken with any other antidepressants. (Some studies show that, if used in certain ways, MAO inhibitors can be combined with antidepressants, and some experienced psychopharmacologists may do this in extremely refractory cases. But this is extremely rare.) Anyone who takes MAO inhibitors must avoid a list of foods and beverages that includes beer, wine (even alcohol-free beer and wine), cheese (except cottage cheese and cream cheese), yogurt, sour cream, raisins, pickled herring, Genoa salami, hard salami, pepperoni, fava beans, avocados, canned figs, soy sauce, caviar, excessive amounts of chocolate or caffeine, and any food that has undergone protein breakdown by aging, pickling, fermentation, or smoking—or that may have undergone protein breakdown by being accidentally spoiled. You have to avoid these foods not only while you are taking MAO inhibitors, but also for at least two weeks after you stop taking them. Eating any of these things while on an MAO inhibitor can cause dangerous, even fatal, increases in blood pressure. Anyone who knows a teenager (or remembers being one) can easily imagine how difficult it would be to keep a youngster on such a dietary regimen.

For the same reason, you also have to avoid many over-the-counter drugs if you are taking an MAO inhibitor, including cold and cough medicines, nasal decongestants, hay fever and sinus medications, weight-reducing and appetite-reducing drugs, and anything containing L-tryptophan. MAO inhibitors can only be used with patients who are reliable and conscientious about medication, and they can't be used by anyone experimenting with illicit drugs, herbal remedies, or any other substance that might cause severe reactions. That they can also cause long-term weight gain makes them a still less attractive option for teenagers. Although the foods listed above cause increases in blood pressure in people using this drug, dizziness from lowered blood pressure, especially when standing up quickly, can also occur on MAO inhibitors. Changes in blood pressure have to be monitored carefully in anyone taking these drugs. For all these reasons, MAO inhibitors are usually used only for patients who do not respond to other drugs.

Nardil and Parnate are the most commonly used of these four MAO inhibitors. Marplan is no longer available in the United States (although it is in Canada), and Eldepryl is only rarely used as an antidepressant.

Nardil (Phenelzine)

The drug comes in 15 mg tablets, and one of these three times a day is the usual starting dose. The dosage is then increased gradually. For many, 60 mg a day for at least four weeks are required before relief is achieved. After the medicine starts to work adequately, the dosage can be reduced gradually. Eventually, a dose as small as 15 mg every other day can be enough to maintain the effect, and this dosage can be continued indefinitely.

Parnate (Tranylcypromine)

The most common undesirable side effect of Parnate is insomnia, which can usually be avoided by taking the last dose before 3 P.M., by reducing the dosage, or by taking a mild sleeping pill along with it. Most of the other side effects—dry mouth, nausea, diarrhea, abdominal pain, constipation, blurred vision, chills, and others— are uncommon or rare. The most dangerous side effect is changes in blood pressure.

The initial dose is 10 mg twice a day, increased to 30 mg a day after three weeks if the desired result has not been achieved. Dosages up to 60 mg a day are sometimes used. This dosage is con- tinued for another week, but after that if there is no improvement, continued use of the drug is unlikely to help. Parnate comes in 10 mg tablets.

Marplan (Isocarboxazid)

Because it can cause changes in heart rhythm and rate as well as other side effects, Marplan is no longer sold in the United States. It is still available, however, in Canada, and for some patients who have failed to respond to other medicine, it can be useful.

The starting dose is 10 mg twice a day, and this can be increased by 10 mg at a time up to 60 mg a day. If there is no beneficial effect within three to six weeks, continued use of the drug will probably not help. The drug comes in 10 mg tablets.

Eldepryl (Selegiline)

Eldepryl is now sometimes used as an antidepressant, although it is officially indicated only for treating the symptoms of Parkinson's disease. As an antidepressant, it must be used in much larger doses than when used to treat Parkinson's disease. It cannot be combined with tricyclic antidepressants or with any of the SSRIs.

ELECTROCONVULSIVE THERAPY

Electroconvulsive therapy (ECT), sometimes called "shock therapy" (usually by those who disapprove of it), has a terrible reputation, but it is a well-tested and proven treatment for depression. In some countries (for example, Great Britain) it is thought of as a first-line treatment since it is more effective—and more rapidly effective—than drug therapy. In the United States, it is usually used only when drug trials have failed. Yet even in these cases, it can be highly effective. ECT has undoubtedly been misused in the past—either for punishment of misbehavior or to treat diseases for which it does not work—and this may be part of what has led to its general condemnation in certain circles. When it was first devised, it was administered without effective anesthesia, which could lead to the consequences of a grand mal seizure—strained muscles, broken bones, and so on. In the United States, four states severely restrict its use. This is unfortunate, because its effect can be dramatically beneficial. ECT is indicated for depression, especially depression with psychotic features (hallucinations or delusions, for example), particularly in suicidal patients and when antidepressant medicine doesn't work. However, it is much more often used with adults than with teenagers.

ECT works by inducing a seizure, similar to the seizures of epilepsy. This is done by giving an electrical stimulus to the brain through electrodes attached to the patient's skull. There are two methods, unilateral and bilateral. In unilateral ECT, the electrodes are attached over the temporal area of the nondominant side of the patient's forehead, and at the top of the skull. For bilateral ECT, both temporal areas are attached. Before administering electroconvulsive treatment, the doctor will take a complete history and do a thorough physical examination. An electrocardiogram will be taken, because the procedure involves the administration of a drug called atropine, which can affect the heart. Guidelines published by the American Psychiatric Association also demand a complete blood chemistry (including blood count, hemoglobin, blood clotting factor, and platelets) and a complete metabolic profile including liver and kidney function tests, urinalysis, and chest X-ray. The patient is connected to an electroencephalogram which is used to monitor the progress of the procedure by recording seizure activity in the brain.

The procedure is often carried out in a recovery room or sometimes in a doctor's office. In most cases, the anesthesia is delivered by an anesthesiologist and not by the psychiatrist who is administering the ECT. The patient lies down on a bed, and an intravenous line is inserted into his or her arm for administering medication. Attached to the other arm is a blood pressure cuff to monitor blood pressure during the procedure. Electrocardiogram leads are also attached to monitor heart rhythm and rate by viewing an overhead screen. A small clip called a pulse oximeter attached to one finger monitors the oxygen content of the patient's blood to help ensure that the procedure is being performed safely.

The patient's forehead is cleaned with alcohol-soaked cotton, and electrical leads are attached with a mild self-adhesive pad or secured around the forehead with an adjustable strap. The other end of the leads is attached to the ECT machine, which generates an electrical current at a controlled rate and in a highly specific way such that it is incapable of administering a dangerous amount of current. Atropine or glycopyrrolate may be given by an injection in the arm before the procedure or through an IV line at the time of the procedure to prevent irregular heart rhythms. Then a short-acting anesthetic is administered to put the patient to sleep. Finally, a muscle relaxant, succinylcholine, is administered through an IV, but prevented from going to the arm muscle by the inflated blood pressure cuff. (Some people metabolize this drug more slowly than others and so will receive artificial ventilation until it wears off.) When the seizure is induced, it can be visually noted and timed by the contraction of the arm muscle—the only muscle unaffected by the muscle relaxant.

After all these preparations are done, an electrical current just large enough to induce a seizure is sent to the patient's brain. This seizure lasts between 20 and 75 seconds, and its progress is monitored on an electroencephalogram which records the electrical impulses produced by the brain. The patient wakes up within a few minutes after the procedure ends. And that's it. Modern ECT bears no resemblance whatever to Hollywood-style portrayals of it in movies such as *One Flew Over the Cuckoo's Nest.*

ECT can have unpleasant side effects, most commonly a bad headache, which usually responds to Tylenol. When ECT is administered bilaterally, short-term memory loss is common—the patient can't remember what happened immediately before and after the treatment. Memory problems are much less common when the treatment is administered to only one side of the brain, but unfortunately some people respond only to bilateral treatment, and those who respond to unilateral treatment often need more sessions of ECT to get the same relief. Much more rarely, people complain of persistent and chronic memory problems after electroconvulsive therapy.

LIGHT THERAPY

Even patients who feel reluctant about medicine or ECT often feel more comfortable with this form of therapy for depression. Here the patient sits in front of special lights of a particular intensity for a certain period of time, usually in the morning. It is effective for people with seasonal affective disorder (SAD), who tend to get more depressed in the winter, and studies are under way now looking at the procedure as a possible safer alternative to medication for pregnant women nursing babies. One of the limitations of this technique was the bulkiness of the required equipment, but now more portable versions of these lights are available.

ALTERNATIVE THERAPIES

Wherever there is a disease that is chronic and difficult to treat, alternative therapies will be tried. There are no alternative therapies for diseases for which we have extremely good conventional treatments. Whoever heard of an alternative therapy for strep throat, for example? No one needs an alternative therapy for such an ailment—we know what causes it, and we know how to cure it with antibiotics. But depression is different. First, it is mysterious in its cause and not always easy to treat effectively. Second, depression is still stigmatized: if a person is taking "only an herb," which he doesn't need a psychiatrist to prescribe, then he can feel he's not really "mentally ill." So people will try herbal medicines and other alternative therapies to find relief, and some will no doubt find them beneficial. Although the National Institutes of Health has now set up a branch to study herbal medicines, there is still little in the

scientific literature to demonstrate the safety or efficacy of these substances. It is also true that the drug companies that spend enormous
amounts of money to study new and patentable drugs are reluctant
to spend money studying herbs that anyone can produce and sell
without a license.

St. John's Wort

St. John's wort, an herb whose scientific name is *Hypericum perfo-
ratum,* is an ancient remedy for insomnia and "the blues." *Wort* is a
Middle English word meaning "plant," a word which survives as the
term for the solution of sugar obtained by infusion from malt and
used to make beer, and in the names of certain plants like figwort.
Recently St. John's wort has gained some popularity as an alternative medicine for treating depression.

Studies of varying scientific quality have been done to determine
if St. John's wort has any effect on depression, and there is some
evidence that it is more effective than placebo. None of the studies,
however, meets the standards for FDA approval. The presumed
active ingredient in St. John's wort is hypericum, which appears to
be similar to MAO inhibitors in its chemical structure. But since
plants contain many chemicals, it isn't clear what the active ingredient in St. John's wort actually is.

Hypericum seems to have few side effects, but there is little data
about long-term safety. St. John's wort is available in pill form,
though purity can vary considerably, since no FDA approval is
required to manufacture or sell the product. It is widely available, in
pill form, as an herbal tea, and as a liquid. It costs between $5 and
$10 for sixty 300 mg capsules. Information on what doses are
appropriate or effective is hard to come by, but studies have been
conducted using daily doses between 300 mg and 1000 mg. There is
no reliable information on the potential of hypericum for interaction
with other drugs.

SAMe

Although SAMe (pronounced "sammy"), whose chemical name is S-adenosyl-l-methionine, has been the subject of much press attention recently, its antidepressant effect has been known for more than twenty-five years. SAMe is a molecule produced by all living cells, and functions in a process called methylation, which affects various body systems, including brain function, where it helps regulate the production of serotonin, melatonin, dopamine, and adrenaline. (It also appears to have some effect in relieving the symptoms of arthritis and may even help restore damaged cartilage.) Although the exact mechanism is unknown, it is clear that SAMe affects the workings of neurotransmitters, and it is undoubtedly this effect that helps relieve the symptoms of depression.

Various studies have found SAMe to be significantly more effective than placebo, and about as effective as tricyclic antidepressants in relieving symptoms. There is no evidence that it is significantly more effective than any prescription antidepressant, however. While it may trigger manic episodes in people suffering from bipolar illness, it has almost no other known side effects. There are no large studies to establish exactly how effective it is and what proper dosages are, so most psychiatrists will still hesitate to recommend its use.

Since SAMe is not a drug, no prescription is required for its use. This means that many people will try it whether psychiatrists recommend it or not. A 400 mg dose can cost anywhere from about $3 up to $18, depending on which brand you buy, and sometimes much larger doses are necessary to have an antidepressant effect. This makes SAMe quite a bit more expensive than even the most expensive SSRI.

If you looked in this chapter hoping to find the single "best drug" for treating depression, you were disappointed. MAO inhibitors and tricyclic antidepressants are now rarely used for teenagers (and not often for adults, either), and the SSRIs and related drugs have generally taken over as the drugs of choice. Few adolescents today will benefit from the older medicines. Yet it is still important to remember that some few individuals will, for various reasons, not find the newer drugs useful. The older medicines still have a role, however reduced, to play in the treatment of depression.

The development of effective drugs to treat depression has revolutionized the practice of psychiatry over the past fifteen or twenty years. Standard practice in treating the illness demands the consideration of such medicines as possible therapy, and competent mental health professionals—psychiatrists, psychologists, social workers, and others—recognize this fact. Sometimes a parent will tell me they feel that psychiatric drugs are a "crutch" or a superficial treatment that will "prevent my daughter from getting at the real root of her problem." Fortunately this happens less and less, as people now begin to realize that psychiatric drugs are not a "crutch" but an essential tool of modern medicine in relieving the painful symptoms of a serious illness.

Brand Name	Generic Name	Usual Dose (mg/day)	Type
Prozac	fluoxetine	20–80	Selective serotonin reuptake inhibitor
Zoloft	sertraline	50–200	Selective serotonin reuptake inhibitor
Paxil	paroxetine	20–50	Selective serotonin reuptake inhibitor
Luvox	fluvoxamine	50–300	Selective serotonin reuptake inhibitor
Celexa	citalopram	20–40	Selective serotonin reuptake inhibitor
Serzone	nefazodone	200–600	Serotonin antagonist reuptake inhibitor
Desyrel	trazodone	150–500	Serotonin antagonist reuptake inhibitor
Effexor	venlafaxine	75–375	Serotonin norepinephrine reuptake inhibitor
Wellbutrin, Zyban	bupropion	75–400	Norepinephrine dopamine reuptake inhibitor
Remeron	mirtazapine	15–45	Tetracyclic
Elavil, Endep, Etrafon, Umbitrol	amitriptyline	50	Tricyclic
Sinequan, Adapin	doxepin	100–300	Tricyclic
Tofranil, SK-Pramine	imipramine	25–100	Tricyclic
Norpramin, Pertofrane	desipramine	25–300	Tricyclic
Pamelor, Aventyl	nortriptyline	50–150	Tricyclic
Vivactil	protriptyline	15–60	Tricyclic
Anafranil	clomipramine	25–250	Tricyclic
Surmontil	trimipramine	50–100	Tricyclic
Asendin (former brand name—now generic only)	amoxapine	100–400	Tetracyclic
Ludiomil (former brand name—now generic only)	maprotiline	100–225	Tetracyclic
Marplan	isocarboxazid	20–60	MAO inhibitor
Nardil	phenelzine	15–90	MAO inhibitor
Parnate	tranylcypromine	30–60	MAO inhibitor
Eldepryl	selegiline	10	MAO inhibitor
Generic only	lithium	600–900	

9

Psychiatric Hospitals: What They're For and What Happens Inside

The idea of going into a hospital is frightening—after all, that's where most people die, don't they?—and anyone who has to go into a hospital gets all of our sympathy and concern. But the idea of going into a psychiatric hospital is, for many, even more frightening, but for a different reason: after all, that's a place for people who are nuts, isn't it? It is worth thinking about why it is that a youngster who goes into a psychiatric hospital doesn't seem to get quite the same degree of sympathy as one who goes into a medical hospital. Often, a pediatrician or general practitioner will send a patient to me saying that although a psychiatric consultation is clearly indicated in this case, with hospitalization a likelihood, "these people don't much like the idea of going to a psychiatrist" or words to that effect. Sometimes it isn't only the teenager who resists hospitalization, but her parents as well.

In fact, hospitalization in a modern well-run psychiatric facility is not something to be feared or ashamed of. On the contrary, it is a place to be treated and to get well. And in some cases of adolescent depression, hospitalization is clearly the best approach to treatment. Whether to hospitalize a youngster is a judgment that must be made by the psychiatrist, the parent, and the teenager together. This is the question that must be answered: "Is outpatient treatment enough to stabilize this youngster, or is more than that needed?" In some cases, the answer is perfectly clear to me. With a suicidal teenager, for example, the treatment will almost always include a stay in the hospital. If a treatment requires careful monitoring—electroconvulsive therapy, for example—inpatient treatment is likely to be the best approach. In other cases, the decision will be less clear-cut.

A teenager who goes into a hospital to have a medical disease treated receives the sympathy of his family, friends, and schoolmates. But when a youngster is hospitalized for a psychiatric illness, people look askance—the kid's a loony, he's been sent to a funny farm, he's crazy. This kind of backward attitude toward psychiatric treatment is unfortunate—and if anyone with a psychiatric disease avoids treatment because of it, that is more than unfortunate. It can be deadly.

There are cases in which nothing but hospitalization works. I had a patient named Lee, a 17-year-old college freshman who was doing poorly in her first year away from home, having tremendous difficulty adjusting to unfamiliar people and places. She would come to see me when she was home for vacations, each time seeming more depressed than the previous visit. But she refused to give in to whatever was bothering her and insisted on returning to school. Back at college, she found herself unable to go to classes, or even leave her room, to the considerable dismay of her friends and housemates. Finally, the school administration insisted that she be sent home.

Being home didn't help. She was still unable to leave the house. We tried various regimens of antidepressants and mood stabilizers, which finally allowed her to attend a day treatment program for a few days. But it was clear that none of our efforts were enabling her to function in the world. She needed constant monitoring of her medication and its side effects in order to find the regimen that would work for her. The only way to do this was for her to be in the hospital. After much discussion, she and her parents agreed that this would be the best course. For Lee, hospitalization was an urgent intervention that quickly helped her get back on the right course.

Often the central issue in deciding on hospitalization is whether or not the youngster is at risk for harming himself or others. If a teenager is either suicidal or assaultive, hospitalization will almost always be the correct choice. Depression, as we have seen, is one of the most important risk factors for suicide, and the best predictor of a suicide attempt is that a previous attempt has been made. These considerations will be foremost in deciding whether to hospitalize a depressed adolescent.

GETTING THE ANSWERS ABOUT HOSPITALIZATION

The American Academy of Child and Adolescent Psychiatry recommends that parents get clear answers to the following questions when hospitalization is suggested:

1. Why is psychiatric inpatient treatment being recommended for our child, and how will it help our child?
2. What are the other treatment alternatives to hospital treatment, and how do they compare?
3. Is a child and adolescent psychiatrist admitting our child to the hospital?
4. What does the treatment program for inpatient treatment include, and how will our child be able to keep up with schoolwork?
5. What are the responsibilities of the child and adolescent psychiatrist and other people on the treatment team?
6. How long will our child be in the hospital, and how do we pay for these services?
7. What will happen if we can no longer afford to keep our child in this hospital, and inpatient treatment is still necessary? Parents should know that anyone under 18 qualifies for Medicaid once their insurance runs out. Most freestanding psychiatric hospitals happily take Medicaid.

8. How will we as parents be involved in our child's hospitalization, including the decision for discharge and after-care
   treatment?

9. Is this hospital approved by the Joint Commission for the
   Accreditation of Healthcare Organizations (JCAHO) as a
   treatment facility for youngsters of our child's age, or will
   our child be on a specialized unit or in a program accredited for treatment for children and adolescents?

10. How will the decision be made to discharge our child from
    the hospital?

11. Once our child is discharged, what are the plans for contin-
    uing or follow-up treatment?

The decision to hospitalize a patient must be accompanied by
clearly stated goals, established by the admitting psychiatrist at the
outset. Both parents and teenagers should be aware of these goals;
aware, that is, of what is to be accomplished during the hospitalization. Usually the aim will be to stabilize the patient in such a way
that outpatient treatment of the illness can continue successfully.
This will mean different things for different patients. For a suicidal
youngster, being convinced that the patient will not harm herself is
the primary goal. Establishing a support system that will insure that
the teenager continues with outpatient treatment after discharge is
also essential. These goals will vary in their details depending on
the patient, but they must be met before discharge from the hospital
is considered.

Hospital stays are usually short. This is partly for economic reasons, of course, but short stays are also desirable for other reasons.
Hospitalization is unquestionably a disruptive event for an adolescent (or for anyone, for that matter) and it is almost always best to
return to life outside the hospital as soon as possible. But if a teenager really needs inpatient treatment, it is not in her interest to avoid

hospitalization, or to leave the hospital before being stable enough to handle life on the outside.

WHEN TEENAGERS SAY "NO" TO HOSPITALIZATION

Some adolescents clearly in need of treatment may nevertheless refuse it. This is particularly true when decisions to enter a hospital are being made. "I'm not nuts, and I'm not going into a nuthouse" may be a typical response, and not only from teenagers. What obligations do parents and doctors have under these circumstances, and how are they to proceed?

Informed consent for treatment is a complex legal and ethical issue faced by all medical specialties (see chapter 10 for a more extensive discussion of this problem). It becomes even more difficult when the patient is a minor. As a legal matter, minors (with the exception, in some states, of certain emancipated minors who are managing their own financial affairs) cannot give informed consent for treatment, and therefore, strictly speaking, parents or guardians must make medical decisions for them. But even though a teenager's consent is not legally required, I've always found that the best approach is to avoid involuntary commitment by persuading the youngster that treatment is in her interest. This is a part of my responsibility as the treating psychiatrist, but the family, provided they share my goals, can help. No one should imagine that teenagers, even psychiatrically ill teenagers, are incapable of understanding such explanations. A depressed teenager, all other things being equal, is as capable as any other teenager of understanding what is in her best interest, and the family and I must present our case for hospitalization clearly and in good faith, concealing nothing about what the treatment can and cannot do. Depression and other mental illnesses do not usually diminish a youngster's capacity to help decide about treatment.

PERSUADING A TEENAGER OF THE NEED FOR TREATMENT

Rina was the daughter of a couple who both had jobs on Wall Street. She had a long history of erratic and self-destructive behavior, and had dropped out of school at 16. Her parents tried every approach to persuading her to change, but her heroin addiction was the last straw. They finally resorted to a kind of "tough love" stance. She had been living on the street or with friends for several months when she finally became convinced that she needed to go into substance abuse treatment. Her parents came to get her, and packed her into the car.

Five minutes after they pulled onto the highway, she insisted that her parents stop the car. They did. She got out, sat on the side of the road, and refused to move. It took the arrival of the state troopers to bring her to the emergency room. This was my first meeting with her.

I saw a fierce but frightened kid, afraid of her own behavior as much as she was of going into a rehabilitation program. During the course of our meeting it became clear to me that she was at the very least depressed, and probably suffering from bipolar illness. I suggested that before going into rehab we hospitalize her for a trial of medication for her psychiatric illness. Rina was radically opposed to the idea, but after much discussion she began to realize that perhaps at least part of her behavior was based not on her personality but on her untreated depression, an illness for which there was medicine. She decided to come into the hospital, a place where, she realized, illnesses can be treated.

First, I tell the patient and the family exactly what the goals of hospitalization are in a way that the youngster can agree with and understand. I'm quite frank about the limitations of treatment as well as its benefits, and honest about the limitations of my own ability to effect a "cure." I'm careful to explain that the patient won't get well quickly or suddenly, but that there will be progress toward relief of the symptoms of depression, and specific ways of measuring that progress, which I will then explain.

Although predictions of dangerousness are unreliable, being dangerous to herself or others is almost always a reason for hospitalization, whether the teenager agrees or not. Obviously, there will be much room for subjective judgments in this area, and many opportunities for mistakes. The current limitations in our ability to predict dangerous behavior virtually assure this.

WHAT HAPPENS DURING PSYCHIATRIC HOSPITALIZATION?

Often the route to the hospital begins in the emergency room; sometimes it will begin in a medical hospital where a youngster has been treated for a suicide attempt. Occasionally the police or other authorities are involved. These kids are often extremely ill, and decisions have to be made quickly. In other words, though there is no need for panic, it is hard to avoid the feeling of urgency that surrounds admission to the hospital.

Sometimes a teenager arrives at a medical hospital after a serious suicide attempt and remembers little about the attempt itself. When a youngster arrives in this condition, the emergency room staff follows whatever protocol is necessary based on what the teenager has done or ingested. A parent will usually be asked to check the contents of the medicine cabinet and bring in any medicine bottles that may have been used. Finding out if alcohol use is involved is also important. If friends or siblings are present, they will usually be questioned about what happened, especially if they have direct knowledge of the events. During the medical hospitalization, once the teenager is awake and alert, it may be necessary to arrange for around-the-clock staff coverage to prevent a still suicidal teen from taking further action. (This is also one of the reasons why transfer to a psychiatric unit is so important—they're set up to be safe for suicidal patients.)

After medical treatment, which may last as little as 24 hours or as long as a week, and once the patient is able to communicate, the psychiatrist is called to evaluate ongoing suicidal thinking and to determine what the treatment plan will be.

A teenager may wake up in an intensive care unit (ICU) with no knowledge of what has happened. Although memories may begin to surface in the course of the interview, the ICU is no place to be confrontational. The most important questions for me to ask revolve around how the patient is currently feeling—that is, does she feel glad to be alive, or does she still wish she were dead? Are there elements of psychotic thinking? Are drugs or alcohol part of the problem? Was there a clear precipitant for the attempt—a fight with a parent, an incident with a boyfriend? Regardless of whether the youngster remembers what happened before she woke up in the hospital, the significance of the events needs to be explored.

Sometimes a teenager is brought to the hospital by friends—he has done something at a party or another social situation that his friends find frightening enough for them to take action. Most teenagers would rather not involve parents in matters like this if they can avoid it, but of course this is not a good course of action. No teenager, or group of teenagers, should have to bear the responsibility for an ill friend. All teenagers should be encouraged to call for help from adults when they think someone is dangerously depressed or otherwise losing control.

If psychiatric hospitalization is required, the teenager can be transferred to a psychiatric facility or the psychiatric ward of the general hospital. Where substance abuse is a factor, an inpatient program that can offer both psychiatric and substance abuse treatment might be recommended.

Psychiatric hospitalization, like any hospitalization, provides care 24 hours a day. A psychiatric ward provides in addition a stable and carefully structured environment, a "milieu," in which patients and staff members with various kinds of mental health training and

experience (psychiatrists, psychologists, nurses, social workers, occupational therapists, and others) cooperate in treatment. Psychiatric
units vary in the kinds of patients treated: some treat psychotic or
manic patients, some treat impulsive patients with personality disorders, and some treat depressed or suicidal patients. In other psychiatric facilities, various kinds of patients will be treated together.
Some wards are locked, some unlocked. All hospitals certified by
the Joint Commission on Accreditation of Healthcare Organizations
are required to have staffing patterns and a physical environment
that prevents patients from harming themselves or others.

For a parent or other concerned relative, doing calm and quiet
research on the hospital, its staff, and its programs may be difficult
or impossible when an emergency hospitalization is required, but
here are some facts that may be useful. Some hospitals specialize in
adolescent treatment or have wards that are set aside for adolescents. These have the advantage that teenagers can identify with one
another and offer the kind of direct and honest feedback that can
have much more impact than anything an adult can say. On the other
hand, some teenagers may function better on a ward where there is
a range of ages, and where older patients may take on nurturing and
supporting roles for needy adolescents. Sometimes a teenager will
respond to one particular nurse or to the family intervention suggested by a particular social worker. I remember one patient, a
bright but somewhat aloof college student with a case of bulimia
complicated by depression. Joanna was unresponsive to most of the
staff, but she developed a rapport with one social worker who was
able to carry on helpful therapy sessions with her and her family.
She had found an ally, an adult who could help her make sense of
her parents' desires and expectations. Given the many opportunities
for developing a satisfactory therapeutic relationship that a good
psychiatric hospital provides, Joanna found what she needed.

If a teenager becomes acutely agitated, out of control, or dangerous to himself or others in a hospital, there is a sequence of interventions designed to prevent serious consequences. The first is
de-escalation techniques. This can include talking to the patient,

offering her a chance to go into a room alone, or offering her medication that she can take voluntarily. If this doesn't work, the next
level of intervention may be medication administered involuntarily
by means of a shot, but only if the youngster is engaging in violent
or self-destructive behavior. This may also occur in conjunction
with placing a patient in a locked quiet room. Until recently, the
most drastic intervention was to put a patient in restraints, a procedure that required continuous direct staff observation from arm's
length and constant monitoring of vital signs. In most jurisdictions,
this is no longer legal. Now patients are placed on close observation
with medication as needed to control violence.

A patient needs a locked ward if she is acutely suicidal or at risk
for leaving the hospital before she is completely ready to do so.
Even though the idea of a locked facility may seem frightening, you
can't take chances with an adolescent who is suicidal. If someone
becomes seriously disturbed in an unlocked setting, staff will monitor the patient 24 hours a day, either at arm's length on the ward or
in an unlocked seclusion room.

Most psychiatric units have rules that govern visitors for teenagers.
Parents certainly can visit unless there is some special reason to for-
bid visits, as in cases of child abuse or disputed custody. Sometimes
an adolescent simply doesn't want to see her parents, a decision that
I may, depending on the case, try to convince parents to accept, at
least temporarily. Friends are usually limited to one or two at a time.
Although socializing is important, once there are more than a few
adolescents visiting at once, things can quickly get out of hand—
that is, become too stimulating for the patient or others on the ward.
It is also important to be sure that visitors are not bringing illicit
drugs to someone who was using them prior to admission.

Throughout the week in a psychiatric hospital, patients participate in various staff-supervised therapeutic and educational activities, discussion groups, and meetings. Nurses provide daily reports,
and attend rounds and conferences, usually two or three times
a week. Staff may also meet for educational activities, seminars
on scientific subjects, and administrative duties. Psychiatric wards

schedule regular community meetings varying from once a week to daily, designed to facilitate communication between patients and staff. The object is to help patients function at their highest possible level and prepare them for discharge.

Treatment goals may be modified during hospitalization depending upon how the patient progresses. The extent to which a patient participates in ward activities and responds to demands placed upon her will be factors in making such modifications.

Sometimes the structure itself is therapeutic. The consistent expectation that a patient will faithfully attend group sessions and ward activities can be helpful to a teenager who, for example, hasn't been going to school or accepting the ordinary demands and responsibilities of teenage life. Often a kid who has been truant in school can nevertheless be persuaded to regularly attend such hospital activities.

Nurses and the paraprofessionals who help them are in many ways the most important staff members in hospital treatment. These are the people who will be with a youngster 24 hours a day, while psychiatrists and other professionals will have briefer and more focused contacts with the patient.

AWAY FROM HOME

John, a 19-year-old college student living away from home for the first time, became severely depressed and was brought home and admitted to the hospital. He stayed in his room and refused even to come to the dining room for meals. He insisted that he was in the hospital for medication, and that that alone would make him "right" and able to resume life at home. In a sense, his family confirmed this: they would come to the hospital, provide him company, bring him food, and generally permit him to function without interacting with anyone else in the hospital. His mother understood the need for him to participate fully in his treatment, and she agreed to stop coming to see him until he began to show some willingness to join in the therapeutic activities that would help him. John began, very reluctantly, to eat his meals in the dining room with the other patients and to participate in group therapy sessions. It was in the context of these group sessions that he was ultimately able to begin addressing the issues of separation from his family that played a role in precipitating his depression in the first place.

INSURANCE COVERAGE FOR PSYCHIATRIC ILLNESS

Reading an insurance policy is no one's idea of a pleasant way to spend an evening, but understanding your insurance coverage may make a large difference in the kind of care your youngster receives. Hospitalization is so expensive that almost no one without insurance of some kind can afford to pay for it for very long. Thus it is essential to understand your insurance, and ask questions about what you can't figure out on your own. There are some plans, you should note at the outset, that will not pay for hospitalization that is the result of a suicide attempt.

Despite considerable efforts by the National Association for the Mentally Ill, the American Psychiatric Association, and others, parity between insurance coverage for medical and psychiatric illnesses has still not been achieved—that is, psychiatric illnesses are in general not covered as generously as medical illnesses. Most people have some sort of managed care arrangement that requires a doctor to discuss with an employee of the insurance company whether the treatment plan is approved for reimbursement. The insurance company employee is usually a social worker or nurse known as a "utilization review manager" or "case manager." This person, using a set of guidelines established by the insurance company, authorizes reimbursement for care proposed by the psychiatrist. If there is a disagreement between the psychiatrist and the case manager about whether a covered service is medically necessary, there will usually be a discussion between your psychiatrist and a physician employed by the insurance company. The two doctors will try to develop a satisfactory plan. If you or your psychiatrist are not happy with the outcome, your psychiatrist can provide your care as he sees fit—but the insurance company will not pay for it. You should be clear on what you can do to appeal the decision of a case manager with whom you and your psychiatrist disagree.

Bringing someone to a hospital emergency room does not guarantee admission to that hospital. First, most admissions must be pre-certified, which means that a patient has to meet the insurer's criteria for hospitalization. Second, the hospital whose emergency room you have arrived at might not have a contract with your insurance company, in which case you will have to go to a different institution.

The treatment review process normally takes place over the telephone, although there may be an exchange of written documents. Some plans demand the entire medical record, which must be sent before any payments are authorized. Even after a treatment is approved, the review process doesn't end. The reviewer will monitor the progress of the treatment, and if the psychiatrist decides that additional treatment beyond what was originally authorized is required, he or she must call the insurance company again to receive authorization for continued care.

ARGUING WITH THE INSURANCE COMPANY

Almost everyone has heard horror stories about insurance companies refusing to cover legitimate medical expenses. You and your teenager don't have to be the victims in one of these stories.

Katie, 15, was admitted to the psychiatric ward of our hospital after a five-day stay in the intensive care unit for an overdose of pills and alcohol. She had developed cardiac complications and required close monitoring until that had cleared. Prior to her overdose, she was in treatment with a psychiatrist and a psychologist for severe depression. Her hospitalization was somewhat lengthy because of the need to change her medications and address her severe hopelessness and despair. During the course of her hospitalization, her case was reviewed every two to three days with her insurance company, which authorized the continuing stay. When the hospital submitted a bill to her parents' insurance company it was told that this was not a reimbursable service because the suicide attempt was deliberate and therefore not covered. The position of the insurance company was, of course, absurd. Suicide attempts are a symptom of an illness: clinical depression. The parents naturally did not accept the insurance company's conclusion. After five months of arguing, the insurance company realized their position was indefensible and paid the bill. This does not mean that the insurance company changed their policy: this kind of fight will be necessary the next time, too.

Most insurance plans include "co-pays," the portion of the bill for which the patient is responsible. You must clarify what your co-pay is for any care undertaken. Even a small percentage of a hospital bill can be a substantial amount of money.

Insurance companies generally limit the number of outpatient visits and the length of hospitalization. You should be clear on what these limits are, and on who decides the limits for your adolescent's case. Often there is a yearly or lifetime dollar limit on mental health coverage, which you also have to know. Managed care companies usually have approved lists of providers—for hospitals, doctors, and other mental health care providers—and you must know which caregivers are on your company's list. It is also important to understand what happens if your hospital, doctor, or therapist is not on the list of approved providers.

Some insurance plans limit the kinds of mental health care they will cover. Will your plan cover outpatient treatment? Home care? Day hospital care? Psychiatric hospitalization? The answers to these questions may determine the kind of care your teenager gets.

None of these questions can be answered during an emergency. First, a hospital is obligated to take care of an emergency situation regardless of a youngster's insurance status. Second, you are in no position to take care of these details in the middle of a process as distressing as the hospitalization of a teenager for depression. In an emergency, the insurance company will be notified after the patient is admitted. If further treatment is needed after the emergency situation is resolved, the psychiatrist will speak to the insurance company. Both you and the hospital will need to deal with the issue as soon as possible. If you don't notify your insurance carrier according to the requirements of your policy, you may have considerable difficulty in getting reimbursed. Don't depend on the hospital to take care of this—the insurance company will hold you, and not the hospital, responsible for the bill.

If the teenager is already in treatment and hospitalization is being considered, then the parents can contact the insurance company and find out what is covered, for how long, and where. The insurance company will also want to speak with the clinician who is recommending hospitalization.

DISCHARGE FROM THE HOSPITAL

How is the decision to discharge a patient from the hospital arrived at? Psychiatric illnesses do not usually have dramatic "cures," so how can you tell when a teenager is ready to go home? And what role does the parent play in the decision to end a period of hospitalization?

Every case is different. Some kids begin demanding to be discharged the minute they set foot in the hospital; others are so relieved to be away from a stressful home or school environment that they'd be happy to stay indefinitely.

It is usually bad practice to simply discharge a youngster from the hospital and send her home with no further treatment. Teenagers often require a period of transition before they resume the demands of normal life. Often a partial hospitalization program—four to five hours a day of group and individual therapy provided on an outpatient basis five days a week—is the best solution. Many school systems offer specialized programs that will take adolescents after hospitalization and offer instruction until they are ready to return to the regular school.

PARTIAL HOSPITALIZATION

Anne's first hospitalization was a nightmare. At 15, she was admitted to an adolescent ward of a free-standing psychiatric hospital for treatment of severe depression and anorexia. She had always been somewhat sheltered, an only child with few friends but intense academic interests. In the hospital, she was frightened by her roommate, who had a much longer and more complicated psychiatric history. Some of the other patients also seemed more disturbed and had histories of drug abuse. She begged to be taken home, and once it was deemed safe to discharge her, she was admitted to a partial hospitalization program that specialized in adolescents. She felt much safer there with a structure that included groups and several hours of schooling. Just being able to go home, sleep in her own bed, and be with peers who had similar issues became major steps in her recovery.

What if you as a parent want your teenager discharged, but the psychiatrist thinks it isn't time yet? Get a second opinion. Most facilities will encourage that in any case. Sometimes the compromise of partial hospitalization will turn out to be the best choice for everyone involved.

Sometimes it's the teenager who presses for release before it's safe to do so. And finally, the insurance company may push for discharge before it is time. Here again, partial hospitalization may be the answer. Often the insurance company will be willing to transfer the inpatient benefit to a partial hospitalization program, sometimes offering to "trade" a day of inpatient care for two or more outpatient visits. This has to be negotiated carefully, and with some assurance that the youngster will not need any further lengthy inpatient hospitalization. Such a discharge plan will often include therapy for the patient, medication management, adolescent group therapy, and family therapy.

Any decision to treat, and especially the decision to hospitalize, has certain legal and ethical dimensions. These issues are complex enough with adults—they're even more complex with adolescents. That's what the next chapter is about.

10

Legal and Ethical Concerns

Teenagers are not little kids, and can't be treated as if they are, but most of them are not really independent adults, either. This raises certain ethical and legal questions in medical care that are important for teenagers and their parents to understand.

CONSENT AND REFUSAL

All patients, adults and kids alike, are entitled to an explanation of their treatment, its risks and benefits, and the possible outcome if treatment isn't undertaken. Once this information is absorbed by the patient, and he then agrees to the treatment, he is said to have given his "informed consent." Usually, this consent is given verbally, but sometimes, especially when hospital procedures are involved, the consent is given formally in writing by signing a statement. This statement can be signed by the patient, if he is competent to do so, or by a family member if the patient is not competent or a minor.

Strictly speaking, teenagers up to the age of 18 are minors, and their parents or guardians can make decisions about treatment for them. In other words, the agreement of a teenager isn't required to begin treatment. In practice, however, treatment of a teenager who does not want to be treated is unlikely to be successful. So I always try to gain the agreement of the youngster before the treatment begins—whether it is legally required or not.

The laws about consent to treatment are designed to protect patients' rights while at the same time making certain that an incompetent person or a minor will receive required care even over his objections. In an emergency, for example, informed consent is not required to begin treatment—a person who is unconscious, badly injured, suicidal, or otherwise incapacitated is not capable of giving informed consent. In such a situation, the person is said to be incompetent.

The legal status of teenagers is a complicated question. Adolescents are often treated by the law neither as children nor as adults. In most states, 18 is considered the age of majority, at which time teenagers are considered adults for almost all purposes. Yet even before they reach that age, they are given considerably more personal liberty than younger children. A teenager younger than 18 who has a baby, for example, is in most states legally able to give that child up for adoption. And teenagers, even young teenagers, are permitted in many states to make various medical decisions for themselves. The most common of these is the decision to use birth control, something that teenagers can do on their own in most states without a parent's consent or knowledge. Teenagers in foster care or judicial custody may fall under the jurisdiction of the state or state courts, which make decisions, medical and otherwise, for them. A youngster who is financially independent of his parents and lives apart from them is usually considered capable of making his own decisions about medical care and other matters.

For minors, the consent of one or both parents is almost always required for medical care. Stepparents, foster parents, and legal guardians all have varying levels of authority in granting consent as well. Yet under many circumstances, minors are able to give consent themselves for medical treatment, sometimes even without the knowledge of their parents. Sometimes the treatment being offered is the deciding factor. Confidentiality in drug and alcohol treatment programs, for instance, is guaranteed by federal law, and minors can consent to enter such programs on their own. Similar rules apply in many states to pregnancy testing, abortion, and contraceptive services, to HIV testing, and—most relevant for our purposes—to inpatient and outpatient mental health care services. These rules vary widely from state to state, and many of them, of course, are controversial. Whatever the legal or political position one takes, however, this much is true: treating a bright 17-year-old in the same way one treats an unconscious person is, on the face of it, a bad idea.

The question of refusal of treatment, a separate issue from the question of the legal ability to consent to treatment, may come up when a youngster must be hospitalized. Most states have two criteria for involuntary hospitalization: the patient must be suffering from a mental disorder, and he must be found to present a danger to himself or others. In such situations, there is no question: a teenager (or an adult) must be hospitalized whether he wants to be or not. The rules for carrying out involuntary hospitalization vary from state to state. Some states require one or more physicians to certify that a person refusing treatment must be hospitalized against his will; in others, the courts make these determinations.

Despite what the law sometimes implies about their lack of competency, teenagers, even as young as 13 or 14, are generally just as capable of understanding their health care as adults are. That is, they are cognitively capable of understanding what disorder they are suffering from, why treatment is advisable, what the treatment will require of them, and the consequences of refusing treatment. On the other hand, you could argue that they are less capable because the emotional issues are different for teens than for adults, that they experience more peer pressure, take more risks, feel more invulnerable, and so on. But in the real world, treatment of a teenager who really doesn't want to be treated is unlikely to succeed, so the youngster who needs treatment must be persuaded that it is necessary. How can you do this?

First, the situation is actually not as common as you might think. The kids I see suffering from depression are in terrible pain, and most of them want help desperately. Still, a few resist, and if the situation comes up, you have to be prepared to deal with it. Parents, of course, can help, and they shouldn't consider bribery beneath them. I've had kids come to see me for three sessions at the end of which they are promised they can go to a concert with friends or be given some other reward. Once a young man was silent and completely uncooperative for most of the first session—and the treatment, as you can imagine, wasn't going anywhere. But I was finally able to engage him by challenging some of his ideas about how he thought about himself. His intellectual curiosity got him started. Sometimes just empathic listening or sympathetic comments can get a youngster talking productively and finding therapy valuable. Most people want to be heard and understood, and if you can convince a teenager that this is his chance to figure things out, to tell someone how he's feeling, to understand why he does the things he does, he'll be receptive. I'll try a group, or family therapy, or recommend a school counselor they know or a therapist recommended by one of their friends. I'm not fussy about the method—the point is to get treatment where treatment is required.

It is also often true that teenagers, despite their vigorous protests, want to be pursued and want to be helped. These kids often feel grateful that they were hospitalized even when at first they didn't really want to be. Yet this is unpredictable: there are kids who are hospitalized for treatment and then resent it, and carry their resentment with them for years. There is no question that psychiatric hospitalization has been abused. Kids who were just being difficult have sometimes been kept for long periods of time in psychiatric hospitals not because they needed treatment, but simply because they were acting out in some way and their parents were finding them hard to handle. This happens less than it used to—and it is not too cynical to believe that this has changed not because the rights of teenagers are suddenly being widely respected, but rather because insurance companies have refused to pay for what amounts to little more than incarceration.

Even though most teenagers still receive care, at least initially, through private therapists' offices, they are sometimes best served for all their health concerns by programs designed especially for them, whether these are school-based or special departments of hospitals or other health care facilities.

CONFIDENTIALITY

Therapists, perhaps even more urgently than other health care professionals, must keep all communications with their patients confidential, as well as any records of the treatment, and even the fact that the treatment is taking place. Unless a patient gives explicit permission for some information to be shared with a third party, this principle must never be violated. Violations of this trust between patient and therapist would make therapy impossible.

But in practice, things are a bit more complicated. First, in most states children up to the age of 18 do not legally enjoy these rights. Parents in fact have a right to know what is happening in their treatment—in fact, parents are in charge of giving permission for the treatment in the first place. If a patient goes to a doctor who employs a bookkeeper or a records clerk, then the patient is implicitly agreeing that certain information about his or her treatment will be available to such people. If she gets a blood test, she assumes that the people performing the test will be aware of the results. If the treatment is being paid for by an insurance company, that company may demand access to the details of the treatment. In some states, a therapist is obliged to reveal to the appropriate authorities threats of violence (and often reveal them to those who are the objects of the threats as well) or other dangerous behavior (suicidal or otherwise). If a doctor suspects child abuse, he is obligated to report it, even if the suspicion grows from information that would otherwise be considered confidential. Custody disputes may require the release of confidential communications. And if a patient initiates legal action against a therapist, rules of confidentiality are suspended.

In general, a private therapist's office will provide more confidentiality than a hospital, if only because in a hospital many more people have access to the youngster's medical records. In a hospital, a team of people, professionals and paraprofessionals, will all see a patient's chart at one time or another. There are, of course, well known and widely respected rules that govern all staff concerning the release of confidential information, but obviously any secret becomes less secret with each new person who learns it.

In the case of teenagers in treatment, things become even more complicated. The tendency now is to lean toward the side of confidentiality, giving adolescents the same degree of confidentiality normally given to adults. Still, parents have a right to know what's going on with their children for reasons ranging from the most obvious and selfish ("I'm paying for this treatment, so I have a right to know what's happening in it, don't I?") to the more subtle and altruistic ("If I know about these things, maybe I can help—the more I know about my child, the better, don't you think?").

The answer to these questions—both of them—is "yes and no." Certainly if an insurance company has a right to know the details of the treatment "because they are paying for it," then surely parents have at least the same right. And it is also true that knowing about your youngster is important and can be helpful. Yet there are exceptions, and not just in psychiatric treatment. For example, a physician can offer treatment to a minor without parental consent in emergencies. In most states, minors can get birth control information and prescriptions without parental consent. In some states, a teenager can get an abortion without a parent knowing about it. Successful psychotherapy may depend on seeing that a teenager's rights to private and confidential communication with her therapist are respected.

Confidentiality: How I Handle It

If a parent brings the teenager in, he or she usually has to wait while I talk to the youngster first. Unless there is some compelling reason to have the parent there during the first discussion, I want to see the teenager alone. After the interview, I explain to the youngster what I think the problem is and what I feel needs to be done about it. Then I tell her that now I'd like to talk to her parents. I ask her whether she wants to be there when I talk to them. If she says no, I tell her exactly what I'm going to tell the parents, and then have the conversation with the parents out of the adolescent's presence.

I put it something like this: "My rule is that I don't tell anyone else what you say to me. I'm not going to tell your parents that you are sexually active, I'm not going to tell them you've smoked grass. And I'm not going to tell them any of the other things you've said to me today. I'm just going to tell them what I think you have—depression—and what we can do to get you feeling better. But there are some things I must tell other people. For example, right now I don't think you're in any danger of harming yourself, but if I ever think you are, I am going to tell your parents that. If I think you're going to harm anyone else—which I don't, and I doubt that I ever will—I'm going to tell them that, too. That's the sort of secret I can't keep. If you're engaging in dangerous behavior like drinking, drugging, having unprotected sex, or suffering from an eating disorder, then I'll work with you to help you, but you will have to tell your parents, or we can tell them together. But if I ever do decide that it's necessary to tell anyone else what you've told me, I'm going to tell you first exactly what I'm going to say, and I'm not going to say anything other than what I tell you I'm going to say." Most kids understand the necessity for these rules, and are willing to accept them. Sometimes teenagers will even ask me to tell their parents what they are doing—they feel the parents will more easily accept it from me than from them.

When I talk to the parents the teenager usually wants to be in the room—if only because they want to be there to correct anything the parent says that they don't think is true. Occasionally, they don't want to be there. If I talk to the parents alone, I don't say anything to the parent except what I told the youngster I would say. If the parent asks questions about confidential matters, I tell them I can't answer them.

I like to have the parents discuss the treatment along with the youngster, always keeping in mind that there are issues of confidentiality that must be respected. I am on the patient's side, and I want that to be clear both to the parents and the child. Yet at the same time, and this is especially true in a hospital setting, the family, along with the rest of the treatment team, is an important part of successful treatment.

SOME FINAL WORDS ON CONFIDENTIALITY

Teenagers need to be assured that, within the kinds of limits described above, the information they give to their therapist is held in confidence. There are many reasons for this. Knowing that it will be a private matter may encourage kids to seek help when they need it. Confidentiality is important once treatment begins as well: kids are naturally more willing to disclose private information if they can be certain that the information won't leave the room. Teenagers are especially sensitive about being different from their peers—if it "gets out" that they're in therapy, this may prove humiliating, even devastating. Finally, respecting a teenager's right to autonomy is a recognition of an essential developmental need, one that neither parents nor health care professionals have a right to ignore.

FURTHER READING

GENERAL BOOKS ON DEPRESSION

Blustein, Jeffrey, Carol Levine, and Nancy Neveloff Dubler, eds. *The Adolescent Alone: Decision Making in Health Care in the United States.* Cambridge University Press, 1999.

Cobain, Bev. *When Nothing Matters Anymore: A Survival Guide for Depressed Teens.* Free Spirit Publishing Company, 1998.

Colarusso, Calvin A., M.D. *Child and Adult Development: A Psychoanalytic Introduction for Clinicians.* Plenum Press, 1992.

Cytryn, Leon, M.D., and Donald McKnew, M.D. *Growing Up Sad: Childhood Depression and Its Treatment.* W.W. Norton, 1996.

Fassler, David G., M.D., and Lynne S. Dumas. *Help Me, I'm Sad: Recognizing, Treating and Preventing Childhood and Adolescent Depression.* Viking, 1997.

Golombeck, Harvey, M.D., and Barry D. Garfinkel, M.D., eds. *The Adolescent and Mood Disturbance.* International Universities Press, 1983.

Ingersoll, Barbara D., Ph.D., and Sam Goldstein, Ph.D. *Lonely, Sad, and Angry: A Parent's Guide to Depression in Children and Adolescents.* Doubleday, 1995.

Klerman, Gerald, M.D., ed. *Suicide and Depression Among Adolescents and Young Adults.* American Psychiatric Press, 1986.

McCoy, Kathleen, Ph.D. *Understanding Your Teenager's Depression: Issues, Insights and Practical Guidance for Parents.* Perigee, 1994.

Oster, Gerald D., Ph.D., and Sarah S. Montgomery, M.S.W. *Helping Your Depressed Teenager: A Guide for Parents and Caregivers.* John Wiley & Sons, 1995.

Slaby, Andrew E., M.D., and Lili Frank Garfinkel. *No One Saw My Pain: Why Teens Kill Themselves.* W.W. Norton, 1996.

SCIENTIFIC ARTICLES

The following articles were useful in preparing this book. Some will prove difficult reading for nonprofessionals, but there is something to be gained by seeing how researchers approach the subject of depression, how they scientifically study its causes and treatment, and how they draw their conclusions.

Epidemiology

Angold, A. Childhood and adolescent depression. I. Epidemiological and aeteological aspects. *British Journal of Psychiatry* 152:601–7, 1988.

Carlson and Kashani. Phenomenology of major depression from childhood through adulthood: Analysis of three studies. *American Journal of Psychiatry* 145:1222–25, 1988.

Kashani et al. Current perspectives on childhood depression: An overview. *American Journal of Psychiatry* 138:143–52, 1981.

Keller and Walters. Epidemiology of DSM-III-R major depression and minor depression among adolescents and young adults in the national comorbidity survey. *Depression and Anxiety* 7:3–14, 1998.

Keller, M.B., et al. Course of major depression in non-referred adolescents: A retrospective study. *Journal of Affective Disorders* 15:235–43, 1988.

Kovacs, M. Affective disorders in children and adolescents. *American Psychologist* 44:209–15, 1989.

Lewinsohn, P.M., Clarke, G.N., Seeley, J.R., Rohde, P. Major depression in community adolescents: Age at onset, episode duration, and time to recurrence. *Journal of the American Academy of Child and Adolescent Psychiatry* 33:6, July/August 1994.

Post, R.M., Rubinow, D.R., Ballenger, J.C. Conditioning and sensitization in the longitudinal course of affective illness. *British Journal of Psychiatry* 149:191–201, 1986.

Ryan, N.D., and Puig-Antich, J. Affective illness in adolescence. In R.E. Hales, A.J. Frances, eds. *American Psychiatric Association Annual Review,* vol. 5. American Psychiatric Press, pp. 420–50, 1986.

Depression and Genes

Dragunow, M., Currie, R.W., Fauk, R.L.M., Robertson, H.A., Jansen, K. Immediate-early genes, kindling and long-term potentiation. *Neuroscience and Biobehavioral Reviews* 43:301–13, 1989.

Post, R.M. Models for the impact of affective illness on gene expression. *Clinical Neuroscience* 1:129–38, 1993.

Silberg, J., Pickles, A., Rutter, M., Hewitt, J., Simonoff, E., Maes, H., Carbonneau, R., Murrelle, L., Foley, D., Eaves, L. The influence of genetic factors and life stress on depression among adolescent girls. *Archives of General Psychiatry* 56 (3):225–32, 1999.

Diagnosis

Birmaher, B., et al. Practice parameters for the assessment and treatment of children and adolescents with depressive disorders. *Journal of the American Academy of Child and Adolescent Psychiatry* 37 (10):63S–83S, supp., 1998.

Ryan, N.D., et al: The clinical picture of major depression in children and adolescents. *Archives of General Psychiatry* 44:854–61, 1987.

Shaffer, D., Gould, M.S., Fisher, P., Trautment, P., Moreau, D., Kleinman, M., Flory, M. Psychiatric diagnosis in child and adolescent suicide. *Archives of General Psychiatry* 53:339–48, 1996.

Strober et al. Phenomenology and subtypes of major depressive disorder in adolescence. *Journal of Affective Disorders* 3:281–90, 1981.

Risk for Depression

Brown, J., Cohen, P., Johnson, J.G., Amailes, E.M. Childhood abuse and neglect: Specificity of effects on adolescent and young adult depression and suicidality. *Journal of the American Academy of Child and Adolescent Psychiatry* 38 (12):1490–96, 1999.

Kovacs, M., et al. Depressive disorders in childhood: II: A longitudinal study of the risk for a subsequent major depression. *Archives of General Psychiatry* 41:643–49, 1984.

Kovacs, M., et al. A controlled family history study of childhood-onset depressive disorder. *Archives of General Psychiatry* 54 (7):613–23, 1997.

Suicide

Beck, A.T., Steer, R.A., Kovacs, M., Garrison, G. Hopelessness and eventual suicide: A 10-year prospective study of patients hospitalized with suicidal ideation. *American Journal of Psychiatry* 142:559–63, 1983.

Bollen, K.A., Phillips, D.P. Imitative suicides. *American Sociological Review* 47:802, 1982.

Brent, D., Perper, J.A., Allman, C.J., et al. The presence and accessibility of firearms in the homes of adolescent suicides: A case-control study. *Journal of the American Medical Association* 266:2989, 1991.

Brent, D.A., Perper, J.A., Goldstein, C.E., et al. Risk factors for adolescent suicide: A comparison of adolescent suicide victims with suicidal inpatients. *Archives of General Psychiatry* 45:581, 1988.

Hendin, H. Psychodynamics of suicide, with particular reference to the young. *American Journal of Psychiatry* 148:1150, 1991.

Hendin, H. Suicide: The psychosocial dimension. *Suicide and Life-Threatening Behavior* 8:99, 1978.

Phillips, D.P., Carstenton, L.L. Clustering of teenage suicide after television news stories about suicide. *New England Journal of Medicine* 315:685, 1986.

Depression and Stress

Ambelas, A. Life events and mania: A special relationship. *British Journal of Psychiatry* 150:235–40, 1987.

Ghaziudinn, M., Ghaziudinn, N., Stein, G.S. Life events and the recurrence of depression. *Canadian Journal of Psychiatry* 35:239–42, 1990.

Golombeck, H., Kutcher, S. Feeling states during adolescence. *Psychiatric Clinics of North America* 13:443–54, 1990.

Post, R.M. Transduction of psychosocial stress into the neurobiology of recurrent affective disorder. *American Journal of Psychiatry* 149:999–1010, 1992.

Williamson, D.E., Birmaner, B., Anderson, B.P., al-Shabbout, M., Ryan, N.D. Stressful events in depressed adolescents: The role of dependent events during the depressive episode. *Journal of the American Academy of Child and Adolescent Psychiatry* 34 (5):591–98, 1995.

Depression and Eating Disorders

Hay, P.J., Hall, A. The prevalence of eating disorders in recently admitted psychiatric inpatients. *British Journal of Psychiatry* 159:562–65, 1991.

Herzog, D.B., Keller, M.B., Sacks, N.R., Yeh, C.J., Lavori, P.W. Psychiatric comorbidity in treatment-seeking anorexics and bulimics. *Journal of the American Academy of Child and Adolescent Psychiatry* 31 (5):810–18, 1992.

Walters, E.E., Neale, M.C., Eaves, L.J., Heath, A.C., Kessler, R.C., Kendler, K.S. Bulimia nervosa and major depression: A study of common genetic and environmental factors. *Psychological Medicine* 22 (3):617–22, 1992.

Depression and Learning Disabilities

Huntington, D.D., Ender, W.N. Adolescents with learning disabilities at risk? Emotional well-being, depression, suicide. *Journal of Learning Disabilities* 26 (3): 159–66, 1993.

Shekim, W.P., Hardin, C., Kashani, K., Hodges, K.K., Cytryn, L., McKnew, D.H. Depression in hyperactive boys. Paper presented at the Annual Meeting of the American Academy of Adolescent Psychiatry, Chicago, 1980.

Depression and Cigarette Smoking

Covey, L.S., Tam, D. Depressive mood, the single-parent home, and adolescent cigarette smoking. *American Journal of Public Health* 80 (11):1330–33, 1990.

Patton, G.C., Carlin, J.B., Coffey, C., Wolfe, R., Hibbert, M., Bowes, G. Depression, anxiety, and smoking initiation: A prospective study over 3 years. *American Journal of Public Health* 88 (10):1518–22, 1998.

Patton, G.C., Hibbert, M., Rosier, M.J., Carlin, J.B., Caust, J., Bowes, G. Is smoking associated with depression and anxiety in teenagers? *American Journal of Public Health* 86 (2):225–30, 1996.

Wang, M.Q., Fitzhugh, E.C., Turner, L., Fu, Q., Westerfield, R.C. Association of depressive symptoms and school adolescents' smoking: A cross-lagged analysis. *Psychological Reports* 79 (1):127–30, 1996.

Wu, L.T., Anthony, J.C. Tobacco smoking and depressed mood in late childhood and early adolescence. *American Journal of Public Health* 89 (12):1837–40, 1999.

Growing Up with Depression

Kandel, D.B., Davies, M. Adult sequelae of adolescent depressive symptoms. *Archives of General Psychiatry* 43:255–62, 1986.

Pine, D.S., Cohen, P., Gurley, D., Brook, J., Ma, Y. The risk for early-adulthood anxiety and depressive disorders in adolescents with anxiety and depressive disorders. *Archives of General Psychiatry* 55:56–64, 1998.

Post, R.M., Weiss, S.R.B. Nonhomologous animal models of affective illness: Clinical relevance of sensitization and kindling. In: G. Koob, C. Ehlers, D.J. Dupfer, eds., *Animal Models of Depression,* Birkhauser Boston, 1989.

Post, R.M., Weiss, S.R.B. Sensitization, kindling and anticonvulsants in mania. *Journal of Clinical Psychiatry* 50:23–30, 1989.

Post, R.M., Rubinow, D.R., Ballenger, J.C. Conditioning sensitization and kindling: Implications for the course of affective illness. In: R.M. Post, J.C. Ballenger, eds., *Neurobiology of Mood Disorders,* Williams & Wilkins, 1984.

Rohde, P., Lewinsohn, P.M., Seeley, J.R. Are adolescents changed by an episode of major depression? *Journal of the American Academy of Child and Adolescent Psychiatry* 33 (9):1289–98, 1994.

The Psychology of Depression

Clarke, C.N., Rohde, P., Lewinsohn, P.M., et al. Cognitive-behavioral treatment of adolescent depression: Efficacy of acute group treatment and booster sessions. *Journal of the American Academy of Child and Adolescent Psychiatry* 38 (3):272–79, 1999.

Elkin, I., Shea, M.T., Watkins, J.T., et al. National Institute of Mental Health treatment of depression collaborative research program: General effectiveness of treatments. *Archives of General Psychiatry* 46:971–82, 1989.

Fava, G.A., Rafanelli, C., Grandi, S., Conti, S., Belluardo, P. Prevention of recurrent depression with cognitive behavioral therapy: Preliminary findings. *Archives of General Psychiatry* 55 (9):816–20, 1998.

Fennig, S., Carlson, G.A. Advances in the study of mood disorders in childhood and adolescence. *Current Opinions in Pediatrics.* 7 (4):401–4, 1995.

Frank, E., Kupfer, D.F., Perel, J.M., et al. Three-year outcomes for maintenance therapies in recurrent depression. *Archives of General Psychiatry* 47:1093–99, 1990.

Frank, E., Kupfer, D.J., Wagner, E.F., McEachran, A.B., Cornes, C. Efficacy of interpersonal psychotherapy as a maintenance treatment of recurrent depression: Contributing factors. *Archives of General Psychiatry* 48 (12):1053–59, 1991.

Hayhurst, H., Cooper, Z., Payke, E.S., Bearnals, S., Ramana, R. Expressed emotion and depression: A longitudinal study. *British Journal of Psychiatry* 171:439–43, 1997.

Inamdar, S.C., Siomopoulos, G., Osborn, M., Bianchi, E.C. Phenomenology associated with depressed moods in adolescents. *American Journal of Psychiatry* 136 (2):156–59, 1979.

Kaslow, N.J., Thompson, M.P. Applying the criteria for empirically supported treatments to studies of psychosocial interventions for child and adolescent depression. *Journal of Clinical Child Psychology* 27:146–55, 1998.

Mufson, L., Fairbanks, J. Interpersonal psychotherapy for depressed adolescents: A one-year naturalistic follow-up study. *Journal of the American Academy of Child and Adolescent Psychiatry* 35 (9):1145–55, 1996.

Schwartz, J.M. Neuroanatomical aspects of cognitive-behavioural therapy response in obsessive-compulsive disorder: An evolving perspective on brain and behaviour. *British Journal of Psychiatry, Supp.* 35:38–44, 1998.

Steinberger, C.B. Teenage depression: A cultural-interpersonal-intrapsychic perspective. *Psychoanalytical Review* 76 (1):1–18, 1989.

Uehara, T., Yokoyama, T., Goto, M., Ihda, S. Expressed emotion and short-term treatment outcome of outpatients with major depression. *Comprehensive Psychiatry* 37 (4):299–304, 1996.

Weisman, M.M. Interpersonal psychotherapy: Current status. *Keio Journal of Medicine* 46 (3):105–10, 1997.

Pharmacology

Emslie, G.J., Walkup, J.T., Pliszka, S.R., Ernst, M. Nontricyclic antidepressants: Current trends in children and adolescents. *Journal of the American Academy of Child and Adolescent Psychiatry* 83 (5):517–28, 1999.

Geller, B., Reising, D., Leonard, H.L. et al. Critical review of tricyclic antidepressant use in children and adolescents. *Journal of the American Academy of Child and Adolescent Psychiatry* 38 (5):513–16, 1999.

Jensen, P.S., Bhatara, V.S., Vitiello, B. et al. Psychoactive medication prescribing practices for U.S. children: Gaps between research and clinical practice. *Journal of the American Academy of Child and Adolescent Psychiatry* 38 (5):557–65, 1999.

Simons, A.D. et al. Cognitive therapy and pharmacotherapy for depression: Sustained improvement over one year. *Archives of General Psychiatry* 43 (1):43–48, 1986.

Thase, M.E., Greenhouse, J.B., Frank, E., Reynolds, C.F., 3rd, Pilkonis, P.A., Hurley, K., Grochocinski, B., Kupfer, J. Treatment of major depression with psychotherapy or psychotherapy-pharmacotherapy combinations. *Archives of General Psychiatry* 54 (11):1009–15, 1997.

RESOURCES

ORGANIZATIONS AND SUPPORT GROUPS

Any quick Internet search turns up dozens of organizations devoted to mental health, many of them of little apparent usefulness to depressed teenagers and their parents. In this listing, we have tried to select national organizations most likely to be helpful to those interested specifically in the problems of adolescent depression. We have included Internet addresses where they are available.

American Academy of Child and Adolescent Psychiatry
3615 Wisconsin Avenue NW
Washington, DC 20016
202-966-7300
www.aacap.org
AACAP publishes an excellent series of on-line pamphlets on child and adolescent psychiatry topics. They also publish one of the major professional journals in the field, *The Journal of the American Academy of Child and Adolescent Psychiatry.*

The American Academy of Pediatrics
141 Northwest Point Boulevard
Elk Grove Village, IL 60007-1098
847-228-5005

Fax: 847-228-5097
www.aap.org

The American Association of Pastoral Counselors
9504A Lee Highway
Fairfax, VA 22031
703-385-6967

American Association of Suicidology
2459 South Ash
Denver, CO 80222
303-692-0985
www.suicidology.org
A nonprofit organization dedicated to the understanding and prevention of
suicide.

The American Board of Examiners in Clinical Social Work
8484 Georgia Avenue, Suite 800
Silver Spring, MD 20910
301-587-8733
One of the two credentialing organizations for social workers. The other is
the National Association of Social Workers, Inc.

The American Board of Medical Specialties
One American Plaza
Evanston, IL 60201
The ABMS publishes the *Directory of Certified Psychiatrists,* which has
biographical data on certified psychiatrists, cross-referenced geographically.

American Mental Health Counselors Association
5999 Stevenson Avenue
Alexandria, VA 22304
703-823-9800

The American Nurses Association
600 Maryland Avenue SW, Suite 100
Washington, DC 20024

American Psychiatric Association
1400 K St. NW
Washington, DC 20005
202-682-6000
www.psych.org
The largest professional organization for psychiatrists, publishers of
many books and journals including *The American Journal of Psychiatry,*
one of the two or three most widely read professional journals for psychiatrists.

American Psychiatric Nurses Association
1200 19th Street SW
Washington, DC 20036-2422
Telephone: 202-857-1133
Fax: 202-223-4579
www.apna.org
The American Psychiatric Nurses Association provides leadership to
advance psychiatric-mental health nursing practice, improve mental health
care for individuals, families, groups, and communities, and shape health
policy for the delivery of mental health services.

American Psychological Association
750 First Street NE
Washington, DC 20036
202-336-5500
www.apa.org
The largest professional organization for psychologists, publishers of
many journals and books.

Anxiety Disorders Association of America
11900 Parklawn Drive, Suite 100
Rockville, MD 20852
301-231-9350
www.adaa.org
ADAA promotes the prevention and cure of anxiety disorders and works to
improve the lives of all people who suffer from them. The association is
made up of professionals who conduct research and treat anxiety disorders

and individuals who have a personal or general interest in learning more
about such disorders.

Association for the Care of Children's Health
19 Mantua Road
Mt. Royal, NJ 08061
Telephone: 609-224-1742
Fax: 609-423-3420
E-mail: acchhq@talley.com
The mission of the Association for the Care of Children's Health (ACCH)
is to ensure that all aspects of children's health care are family-centered,
psychosocially sound, and developmentally appropriate. ACCH believes
health care systems and practices are most effective when they are
planned, coordinated, delivered, and evaluated through meaningful collaboration among families and professionals across all disciplines.

Center for Mental Health Services
P.O. Box 42490
Washington, DC 20015
800-789-CMHS (2647)
www.mentalhealth.org
A service of the Substance Abuse and Mental Health Services Administration of the federal government. Publications and information about mental
health.

Depression and Related Affective Disorders Association (DRADA)
Meyer 3-181
600 North Wolfe Street
Baltimore, MD 21287-7381
410-955-4647, Baltimore, Md.
202-955-5800, Washington, D.C.
www.med.jhu.edu/drada
Their mission is to alleviate the suffering arising from depression and
manic depression by assisting self-help groups, providing education and
information, and lending support to research programs. They work in
cooperation with the Department of Psychiatry at the Johns Hopkins University School of Medicine.

Federation of Families for Children's Mental Health
1021 Prince Street
Alexandria, VA 22314-2971
Telephone: 703-684-7710
Fax: 703-836-1040
E-mail: ffcmh@crosslink.net
www.ffcmh.org
Provides information and engages in advocacy regarding research, prevention, early intervention, family support, education, transition, and other services needed by children and youth and their families.

Freedom From Fear
308 Seaview Avenue
Staten Island, NY 10305
Telephone: 718-351-1717; 800-64-PANIC
Fax: 718-667-8893
Freedom From Fear is a not-for-profit organization acting as advocate for those suffering from anxiety and depressive disorders.

International Society for Adolescent Psychiatry
730 Soundview Avenue
Bronx, NY 10473
718-542-0394

Lithium Information Center
7617 Mineral Point Road, Suite 300
Madison, WI 53717
608-836-8070
www.healthtechsys.com/mimlithium.html

MCHB Maternal and Child Health Bureau
Office of Adolescent Health
5600 Fishers Lane, 18A-39
Rockville, MD 20857
Telephone: 301-443-4026
Fax: 301-443-1296
www.mchb.hrsa.gov

Part of the Health and Human Services Administration of the federal government. A rich source of free information and publications about children's health.

National Alliance for the Mentally Ill
200 N. Glebe Road, Suite 1015
Arlington, VA 22203
703-524-7600; 800-950-NAMI
www.nami.org
The largest, and probably most effective, lobbying organization for the mentally ill. NAMI has affiliates in every state, the District of Columbia, the Virgin Islands, Puerto Rico, and American Samoa.

National Association of Social Workers, Inc.
750 First Street NE, Suite 700
Washington, DC 20002-4241
Telephone: 202-408-8600
Fax: 202-336-8311
TTD: 202-408-8396
www.socialworkers.org
The National Association of Social Workers (NASW) is the larger of the two social work credentialing organizations. It publishes the NASW Register of Clinical Social Workers, a listing of social work practitioners. The other social work credentialing organization is the American Board of Examiners in Clinical Social Work.

National Association of State Mental Health Program Directors
Hall of States, 401-444 N. Capitol Street NW
Washington, DC 20001
703-739-9333
www.nasmhpd.org
The National Association of State Mental Health Program Directors (NASMHPD) aims to reflect and advocate for the collective interests of state mental health authorities and their directors at the national level. NASMHPD analyzes trends in the delivery and financing of mental health services and builds and disseminates knowledge and experience reflecting

the integration of public mental health programming in evolving health care environments.

The National Center for the Study and Prevention of Suicide
Washington School of Psychiatry
1610 New Hampshire Avenue NW
Washington, DC 20009

National Clearinghouse for Alcohol and Drug Information
P.O. Box 2345
Rockville, MD 20847-2345
301-468-2600; 800-729-6686
www.health.org
A part of the federal government's Substance Abuse and Mental Health Services Administration.

National Clearinghouse on Family Support and Children's
Mental Health
800-628-1696
www.rtc.pdx.edu/resource/clearing.htm
Provides publications on parent/family support groups, financing, early intervention, various mental disorders, and other topics concerning children's mental health. Also offers a computerized databank and a state-by-state resource file. Recording operates 24 hours a day.

National Depressive and Manic Depressive Association
730 N. Franklin, Suite 501
Chicago, IL 60610
800-826-3632; 312-642-0049
www.ndmda.org
NDMDA is a patient-run, grass-roots organization with 275 chapters offering support and advocacy for those with depression and bipolar disorder. Their mission is to educate patients, families, professionals, and the public concerning the nature of depressive and manic-depressive illness as treatable medical diseases; to foster self-help for patients and families; to eliminate discrimination and stigma; to improve access to care; and to advocate for research toward the elimination of these illnesses.

The National Foundation for Depressive Illness, Inc.
P.O. Box 2257
New York, NY 10116-2257
800-245-4306; 800-248-4344
Toll-free hotline which plays a recorded announcement about symptoms and treatment.

The National Institute of Mental Health
6001 Executive Boulevard
Bethesda, MD 20892-9663
E-mail: nimhinfo@nih.gov
www.nimh.nih.gov
The National Institute of Mental Health (NIMH) is part of the National Institutes of Health (NIH), the principal biomedical and behavioral research agency of the United States Government. NIH is part of the U.S. Department of Health and Human Services. The Web site of the NIMH provides a wealth of information about mental health and offers numerous brochures, manuals, and other publications.

National Institute of Mental Health (NIMH)
Depression Awareness, Recognition, and Treatment
(D/ART) Program
5600 Fishers Lane, Room 10-85
Rockville, MD 20857
800-421-4211; 301-443-4140
A special program on depression run by the National Institute of Mental Health.

National Mental Health Association
1021 Prince Street
Alexandria, VA 22314-2971
Telephone: 703-684-7722
Fax: 703-684-5968
Mental Health Information Center: 800-969-NMHA
TTY line: 800-433-5959
www.nmha.org

Provides brochures on clinical depression, the warning signs of illness, and on women and stress. Offers additional assistance and a referral service to mental health organizations. Makes referrals to mental health groups.

National Mental Health Consumers' Self-Help Clearinghouse
1211 Chestnut St., Suite 1000
Philadelphia, PA 19107
Telephone: 800-553-3549
Fax: 215-636-6310
E-mail: thekey@delphi.com
www.mhselfhelp.org
The Clearinghouse is a consumer-run national technical assistance center established in 1986 and funded by a grant from the Federal Center for Mental Health Services. They are committed to helping mental health consumers improve their lives through self-help and advocacy and help consumers plan, provide, and evaluate mental health and community support services. They supply a lot of useful information through pamphlets, toolkits, manuals, and a newsletter, *The Key*—all focused on mental health and consumer issues.

National Organization for SAD (Seasonal Affective Disorder)
P.O. Box 40133
Washington, DC 20016
A support group for SAD patients and their families.

The National Register of Health Service Providers in Psychology
1730 Rhode Island Avenue NW, Suite 1200
Washington, DC 20036
202-833-2377
Licensed psychologists with at least two years of supervised experience are listed in this register. Listing here does not, however, guarantee experience in psychotherapy.

INDEX

ABOUT THE AUTHORS

MAUREEN EMPFIELD, M.D., is Director of Psychiatry at Northern Westchester Hospital Center in Mt. Kisco, New York, and Assistant Clinical Professor of Psychiatry at Columbia University College of Physicians and Surgeons. She is the author or coauthor of more than a dozen book chapters and articles for professional journals.

NICHOLAS BAKALAR is a New York–based writer and editor who is the author or coauthor of eleven books on a variety of subjects.